Baby *talk*

P9-EGM-783

DCLS/LOGAN BRANCH
498 BECKETT ROAD
LOGAN TWP., NJ 08085

Baby *talk*

A Guide to Using Basic Sign Language to Communicate with Your Baby

Monica Beyer

Jeremy P. Tarcher/Penguin
a member of Penguin Group (USA) Inc.

JEREMY P. TARCHER/PENGUIN
Published by the Penguin Group

Penguin Group (USA) Inc., 375 Hudson Street, New York,
New York 10014, USA

Penguin Group (Canada) 90 Eglinton Avenue East, Suite
700, Toronto, Ontario M4P 2Y3, Canada (a division of
Pearson Penguin Canada Inc.)

Penguin Books Ltd, 80 Strand, London
WC2R ORL, England

Penguin Ireland, 25 St Stephen's Green, Dublin 2, Ireland
(a division of Penguin Books Ltd)

Penguin Group (Australia), 250 Camberwell Road,
Camberwell, Victoria 3124, Australia
(a division of Pearson Australia Group Pty Ltd)

Penguin Books India Pvt Ltd
11 Community Centre, Panchsheel Park,
New Delhi–110 017, India

Penguin Group (NZ), Cnr Airborne and Rosedale Roads,
Albany, Auckland 1310, New Zealand
(a division of Pearson New Zealand Ltd)

Penguin Books (South Africa) (Pty) Ltd
24 Sturdee Avenue, Rosebank,
Johannesburg 2196, South Africa

Penguin Books Ltd, Registered Offices
80 Strand, London WC2R ORL, England

Copyright © 2006 by
The Ivy Press Limited

This book was conceived,
designed, and produced by
The Ivy Press Limited
The Old Candlemakers
Lewes, East Sussex BN7 2NZ, UK

All rights reserved. No part of this book may be
reproduced, scanned, or distributed in any printed or
electronic form without permission. Please do not
participate in or encourage piracy of copyrighted materials
in violation of the copyright holder's rights. Purchase only
authorized editions.

Published simultaneously in Canada

Most Tarcher/Penguin books are available at special
quantity discounts for bulk purchase for sales promotions,
premiums, fund-raising, and educational needs. Special
books or book excerpts also can be created to fit specific
needs. For details, write Penguin Group (USA) Inc.
Special Markets, 375 Hudson Street,
New York, NY 10014.

An application to register this book for cataloging has been
submitted to the Library of Congress

ISBN 1-58542-517-6

Creative Director: PETER BRIDGEWATER
Publisher: JASON HOOK
Editorial Director: CAROLINE EARLE
Art Director: SARAH HOWERD
Senior Project Editor: HAZEL SONGHURST
Designer: JANE LANAWAY
Illustrator: MARK JAMIESON

Printed in China
1 3 5 7 9 10 8 6 4 2

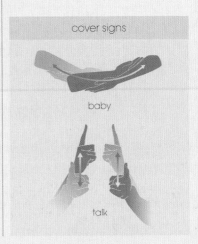

cover signs

baby

talk

Publisher's Note

While the author has made every effort to provide accurate
Internet addresses at the time of publication, neither the
publisher nor the author assumes any responsibility for
errors, or for changes that occur after publication. Further,
the publisher does not have any control over and does not
assume any responsibility for author or third-party websites
or their content.

Author's Note

In this book, I alternate between baby boys and baby girls
and speak of mothers and fathers as primary caregivers.
However, feel free to mentally adjust for your personal family
situation. Also keep in mind that babies vary in their speed
and ability to learn as much as they do physically, and if
you ever have any developmental questions or concerns,
please consult your child's physician.

Contents

foreword   6
introduction   8

1   what to expect from signing   14
2   getting started   18
3   first signs   24
4   troubleshooting   40
5   signing with caregivers   46
6   developing signs   52

7   sign combinations and sentences   70
8   taming tantrums   76
9   advanced signs   82
10 signing and the older child   114
11 branching out   120

further information   126
index   127
acknowledgments   128

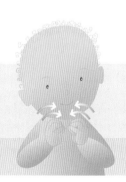

foreword

By Alan Greene, M.D..FAAP

I've been a fan of signing with babies for years. As a pediatrician, when I settled in to read *Babytalk* I had questions in mind. Are the book's ideas about teaching basic sign language to babies developmentally and age appropriate? Are the instructions easy to follow? Would I recommend this book to parents and caregivers in my own practice? The answer is yes!

What's more, I found myself thinking "This looks fun." As parents, you want to do all the right things. We become so busy, however, that sometimes having fun gets lost in our long lists of "must-dos." The beauty of *Babytalk* is that it rolls cognitively and physically stimulating play, communication, and bonding into the same activity. Importantly, it's an activity that you and your child can take at your own pace. As author Monica Beyer makes clear, teaching your baby sign language is not about power-parenting, it's another loving way to interact.

Your baby uses body language to communicate with you from day one. One of the most fulfilling "firsts" is that "ah-ha" moment you recognize what your baby is trying to tell you. "Yes!" you think with love and relief. "We're communicating."

Teaching your baby sign language is a way to extend and refine his or her own nonverbal talk. Your baby will discover many things he or she wants to express before being able to verbalize them fully. With consistency and patience, through sign language you can help your baby bridge the communication gap that occurs while speech develops. On your communication journey, there's no way to avoid misunderstandings and upsets altogether. However, if by learning this beautiful, fluid language you achieve a higher level of communication and allay even a small amount of parent–child frustration—and you have fun together—what a great idea!

In *Babytalk* Monica Beyer takes this great idea and makes it easy to understand. She explains the process in a clear, warm way, with just enough repetition of the key points to reassure parents: "Yes, my baby and I are doing this right." She takes you from first steps that focus on early

Need-Based Signs (milk, eat, more) and High-Impact Signs (mother, father, dog) to more advanced signing for toddlers onward. She quotes enough experts to show that the book is based on a solid foundation without letting technical talk distract from the process or the fun.

Throughout the book you'll find helpful stories from signing parents including the author and her daughter, Lauren. These real-life stories will amaze and inspire you, and collectively they offer a balanced benchmark for realistic expectations.

Learning sign language is a journey your whole family can make. You and your baby learn your first handful of signs. The family is curious. You explain. Soon, siblings, grandpa, and other important caregivers join in: "Let's eat," "Cookies, Dad," "Grandma, I love you." No one is ever too old for a little *Babytalk*.

So, settle in and enjoy the process—it's good for you.

ALAN GREENE, M.D., FAAP
Author *From First Kicks to First Steps* and *DrGreene.com*.
Division of General Pediatrics, Lucile Packard
Children's Hospital at Stanford University.

Introduction

signing with babies

Signing with babies—is it the new fad? Something only power moms who want superbabies do? A surefire way to form a speech delay? You may already know that the answer to all of the above questions is a resounding NO!

People have been signing with their babies for years. The most common reason for doing so is an intense desire on the part of a parent or caregiver to find out exactly what is going on in a baby's mind—what does she need? What does she want? What does she observe? What does she think about and remember?

natural expression

Infants develop the fine muscles in their hands before they develop those required for speech, so they're equipped to communicate with you before they can speak. Most babies will invent their own "signs" to get their meaning across. A baby may learn to wave bye-bye, for example, or point to her nose when it needs a wipe. These symbolic gestures are one form of communication used by preverbal infants. In addition to pointing and grunting, a baby has the potential use of her hands and body to help her communicate.

It is easy to encourage and expand this natural form of communication. Signing with babies isn't difficult, and it has been proven through years of research to be beneficial to speech acquisition. It is fun, inspirational, and downright amazing.

it's your choice

As a mother of three children I learned to sign with my infants, drawing on the experiences of other baby-signing parents. After viewing a TV program on signing with babies, I thought I would give it a try. As my first signing baby demonstrated advanced thoughts and feelings, I was convinced that it was an excellent parenting choice. At the time, there was little information available on signing with babies, so I developed my website to help other parents sign with their own babies.

"See the bird, Mommy?"
Sharing what excites
her is just one benefit
of signing.

shared experiences

Parents everywhere are effectively communicating with their babies using sign language. Imagine your baby being able to share with you that she needs a diaper change or would like a cup of juice, or that her ears are hurting, or that she sees a bird over on the tree. Nonsigning children commonly cry, fuss, whine, point wildly, or grunt their desires, leaving you, as a parent, to decipher these gestures based on tone or intensity. By introducing sign language, your child will gradually associate signs with activities or favorite objects, which will not only reduce her frustrations but yours as well.

Getting started is not a huge time-consuming chore, all you need is the knowledge of just a handful of signs, along with a healthy dose of motivation, consistency, some guidance, and a few basic tips. Keep in mind that babies vary in their speed and ability to learn. If you have any developmental concerns, please consult your child's physician.

myths about signing with babies

Signing causes speech delays.
According to experts, as well as countless parents who have signed with their babies, the answer is "No." Using sign language can actually spur verbal development and is even recommended by speech/language pathologists for children with a speech disorder or delay.

Signing with your child will create a genius superbaby.
Of course not. You simply want to be able to communicate before your baby can speak.

Signing with babies takes a great amount of time and effort.
Signing with your baby can become a natural process, accenting your everyday conversations with your child, and you only need to learn the signs a few at a time—just as your baby does.

using American Sign Language

I highly recommend using a formal signed language (such as American Sign Language—ASL) when signing with babies. There are a number of reasons for this. The most common reason cited by professionals, caregivers, and parents is that if you use signs from an already established language it is easier to communicate with others who are also using sign language. This may be a deaf relative or friend or even other babies who are signing with their parents. Even though signs can vary widely from region to region (even more so from country to country) the signs are often consistent enough to be considered a standard. You will have a ready resource to learn signs from, as opposed to creating your own signs.

the same language

Almost all baby sign-language products and TV programs are based on ASL, and carers in U.S. daycare centers are increasingly adopting baby signing using ASL. They find that it helps the children to communicate clearly at an earlier age.

accuracy is the key

One common myth that you might hear about signing with babies is that ASL is somehow far too complex for little hands to form. Keep in mind that we are encouraged to talk to our babies using regular speech rather than infantile words—we are to provide a clear and accurate model for verbal communication. Babies will not speak accurately at first, but they will eventually refine their speech and speak correctly. The same holds true for signing with babies. They may not accurately sign back to us in the early months, but as they grow and their fine motor skills become more developed, they will correctly sign a word.

On the other hand, I also believe that it is reasonable and sometimes necessary to create signs in cases where you absolutely are not able to find the correct sign in a book or a website. For example, I was unable to find a sign for Teletubbies when my son was signing, so I made one up (finger twirling above the head, signifying Laa Laa's head decoration).

"Communication, like physical contact, is an essential component in our children's development. We can benefit from the powerful gift the deaf have given us. That gift is actually a treasure waiting to be unlocked. And the key to that treasure is in your hands."

Dr. Joseph Garcia, *Sign with Your Baby*

signed languages around the world

American Sign Language (ASL)

British Sign Language (BSL)

Australian Sign Language (Auslan)

Langue des Signes Québécois (LSQ)

Langue des Signes Française (LSF)

Lenguaje de Signos Mexicano (LSM)

Lengua de Signos Española (Mimica)

These are just a few of the many signed languages used in countries around the world. If you live in an area different from those listed above, you might check with your local deaf community to see what resources are available for a particular signed language. Regardless, ASL is always an option if you have access to a computer, because there are several good ASL dictionaries online *(see page 126)*.

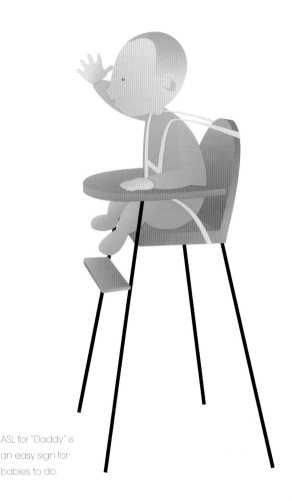

ASL for "Daddy" is an easy sign for babies to do.

research behind signing with babies

While it may seem like a brand-new trend, signing with babies actually began about seven years ago. Even before then, deaf families, speech language pathologists, and child development experts signed with preverbal infants. Some remarkable results were produced by academic research studies, and one research group (Acredolo and Goodwyn) had a hand in bringing signing with babies into the public eye.

Dr. Linda Acredolo and Dr. Susan Goodwyn, founders of Baby Signs, Inc., have conducted more than 20 years of research on this subject. Their findings showed that babies who were exposed to signing not only scored higher in standardized language tests than babies who did not sign but that they scored an average of 12 points higher on intelligence tests at eight years old.

"Eat" may be one of your baby's first signs—and one of your baby's first words!

"Having worked directly with literally thousands of children, and having carefully studied the language development of hundreds of them for our research, I can say with confidence that signing is not in any way associated with delayed speaking."

Dr. Michelle Anthony

signing smart

Dr. Michelle Anthony, codeveloper with Dr. Reyna Lindert of the Signing Smart program, has this to say about signing and speech development: "Learning to talk is a biologically pre-wired ability. No child can 'choose' not to talk because they can sign or because they are comfortable with alternative modes of communication. It would be like saying, 'I have decided I will not grow an inch this year. I am comfortable with my height the way it is, so I will just will it on myself to not grow another inch over this year.' Children cannot physiologically do this—choose to not grow an inch—any more than they can choose not to learn to talk."

language development

In 2005, a study conducted by the University of California at Berkeley was presented at the Annual Convention of the American Psychological Association in Washington, D.C. This paper highlighted some of the research by Dr. Anthony,

Dr. Reyna Lindert, and Dr. Diane Anderson. They had discovered that children who utilized sign language, in combination with specific interaction strategies developed by Signing Smart, do not have any delays in language development. In fact their research demonstrates that these children are likely to experience an improvement of overall language production compared to nonsigners.

signing on the big screen

Have you seen *Meet the Fockers*? This major Hollywood movie has a very special baby who is not only learning sign language but happily and easily demonstrates it. The movie not only gave exposure to signing with babies in general but was really inspiring—it is one thing to hear about signing, but another thing altogether to see it happen.

1 what to expect from signing

advantages and hints

There are many advantages to signing with babies. The main benefit is the higher level of communication you will achieve. You will be giving your child a tool for communication before he is physically able to speak. You will be able to experience the world from your baby's eyes and fulfill his needs with greater ease. There will no longer be so many guessing games on your part and there will be less frustration all round.

Here are a few important points to remember before you start signing with your baby:

BE CONSISTENT Use the same sign the same way for the same action or object. This will help your baby become familiar with the sign and he will be able to sign it back to you sooner. Don't kill yourself trying to learn an entire signed language in a week, however. Concentrate on a handful of signs at first and build from there.

BE OPEN TO INTERPRETATION Babies will not always make a sign correctly the first time they sign it, just as they won't be able to say a word correctly the first time they speak it. Keep signing the word the correct way and your baby will soon grow more accurate.

BE OPEN TO SUGGESTION Sometimes a baby will create a sign for himself. Feel free to continue using it and applaud his creativity. Keep in mind, though, that you can also easily adapt an invented sign to a more formal sign (such as the ASL version). Acknowledge your child when he uses his own sign and model back with the ASL version. He will soon correct himself.

BE EXPRESSIVE Use your face and body in addition to your hand signs. You should also say the word as you sign it. Alter the tone of your voice depending on the context. Make it sound fun and interesting.

Discuss signing with the rest of the family and get them on board with the project if you can.

"I have been teaching my daughter ASL for four or five months now. About three weeks ago she had a signing explosion. She went from signing 15 signs regularly to now just over 40 signs."

Kris, mother of Rachel, 14 months

Big sister signing "milk" with her brother is not only fun but motivating as well.

suggested timeline for signing

6–9 months Introduce some need-based and high-impact signs

7–12 months Your baby will probably start signing back

12 months onward Introduce secondary signs

Around 2 years Your child may start to combine signs and may combine signs and speech

Remember that these are suggestions, not rules.

do you need to know all of ASL?

A common question many parents ask is, "Do I need to learn the entire language of ASL?" The easy answer is "No." Unless you already know ASL or have a hearing-impaired or deaf child, you will need to learn only a handful of signs at a time. Most parents learn to sign alongside their baby.

how it happens

When you start signing with your baby, you can expect his sign acquisition to mimic spoken language acquisition. There are a few phenomena to watch out for.

Expect your child to recognize a sign that you are making well before he starts using it on his own. Recognizing words and signs is called receptive language, and being able to form words and signs is called expressive language. You can expect your child to go through the former stage before going through the latter, both in signing as well as in speech.

What toy to play with? The sign for "ball" eliminates the guessing game on your part!

"My four-month-old son definitely recognizes the signs for milk and diaper change. He gets really excited at the milk sign and his whole body jigs around and a huge smile comes over his face. If I'm changing his diaper in a new place and sign 'diaper change' he relaxes straight away as if he knows what is going to happen."

Gill, mother of Finlay, 4 months, and Sophie, 2$^1/_2$ years

is it a sign?

Signs that have a similar handshape will often start out the same. In other words, your baby may appear to be making the same sign for several words. Some that I noticed were "ball," "more," and "hurt." They all are two-handed signs where the hands are brought together. This can be compared to a child saying "ba" for several words, such as "ball," "bird," and "balloon."

This is all perfectly normal. Your challenge is to figure out what your baby is trying to tell you, using the context. If you're feeding your child, he might want more, but if he's playing, he might want his ball. Of course, this may be easier said than done and you may still be mystified. In this case you will have to give your baby more time to produce more clear-cut signs.

keep on talking

When your child first starts signing, he may use one sign for everything. Just as children will use one word (like "mama") for many things, so too will children use one sign for many things. This is a good thing. This means that he has realized that the gestures do indeed stand for something and they can be used to obtain it. Instead of becoming flustered because your baby seems to be signing meaninglessly, be happy that he's getting it. Continue showing him other signs, remain consistent, and he'll eventually begin to use the proper sign in the proper context.

You can expect what I like to call a "signing explosion." It seems that after mastering several signs, most babies suddenly realize that signing will get them what they desire and their ability to soak up signs like a sponge becomes evident. My son went through this, and I couldn't supply him with signs fast enough. I recognized the look he would give to me, that questioning look as he viewed a new object or activity and wanted to know the sign—because he wanted to be able to communicate about it.

2 getting started

the basics

"Milk" is one of the most popular signs to get started with, and with good reason. It is a sign for one of your child's most basic needs—being fed—which not only nourishes her body, but gives comfort, warmth, and happiness as well as building trust.

The first step to signing with your baby is picking the signs you want to begin with. Flip through the First Signs chapter and select a handful. You might choose to begin with only one sign, but I recommend that you start with several. Most parents choose first signs that involve eating, such as "milk," "eat," or "drink." Add a couple of really fun or interesting signs, such as "dog," "bath," or "fan."

time it right

Show your child the sign directly before, during, or directly after an activity. For example, during nursing, if you choose to begin with "milk," or as you're spooning baby cereal in the general direction of your baby's mouth, if you choose to begin with "eat."

Use the signs before or during the activity, and continue to show your baby the sign often. Consistency is the key, but you don't have to sign it every single time—just often enough so that she begins to get the picture.

Use your selected signs until your baby begins to sign back to you, then choose another sign and start the process over again—but don't stop showing the signs she already knows. Once you begin adding signs like this you will find your sign vocabulary really grows and you truly are learning right along with your child.

The more signs your baby knows, the easier it will be for her to pick them up, especially once she realizes that she can get her needs taken care of and her wants fulfilled by using signs. Soon you will become really comfortable using the signs and they will become second nature to you.

> "Initially, everyday simple activities and needs such as eating, drinking, changing diapers, or wanting more of something are perfect opportunities to introduce signs."
>
> Dr. Joseph Garcia, *Sign with Your Baby*

need-based signs and high-impact signs

Need-Based Signs are those signs that reflect a baby's needs. Anything dealing with sustenance, comfort, warmth, sleep, and safety would fall in this category. High-Impact Signs are signs connected to objects, activities, or situations that you know your own baby finds highly interesting or extremely fun.

getting your baby's attention

It is common for a baby not to look at the signing adult who wishes to sign with her. Her attention may be distracted by whatever she is looking at—and by what you wish to teach her to sign about. Use a tip from Dr. Michelle Anthony and Dr. Reyna Lindert: use the sign in front of or on the object you are signing about. You can even sign it on your baby's body!

Lights are so exciting! This is a good example of a High-Impact Sign. Many babies are fascinated by lights, and if yours is, make it one of her first signs.

reading your baby's cues

Now that you know the basics, you will want to know the specific indications that your baby is indeed ready to sign. There are many parents who choose to sign from birth, while others don't find out about signing until their child is over one year old. The truth is that there is no magic age to begin signing, so it can be tricky finding the right time to begin introducing signs.

sitting up alone

Many babies don't express any interest in signing until they are sitting up. Once a child has mastered sitting up on her own, without supporting herself with her hands, she may not only be more receptive to viewing the signs you make but also more capable of signing back on her own. It is normal for babies to learn to sit up between six and nine months of age. After the monumental physical task of learning to sit is accomplished, they may be able to focus on a different skill set, such as communicating through signing.

action and reaction

You will also want to observe your baby and see if she is showing interest in what you are doing with your hands. Does she show excitement when you unbutton your blouse for nursing or prepare a bottle? Also take notice of how she reacts to her surroundings. Do her eyes follow the family dog around the room? Does she seem to notice the sounds of her daily routine? For example, does she begin to wiggle happily at the sound of water being run for a bath or noticeably light up when daddy opens the front door? These are all good indications that your baby would welcome some assistance in communication. Remember, you will want to focus on need-based activities as well as objects, people, or activities that are really interesting or a lot of fun—in other words, things your baby will be keen to sign about.

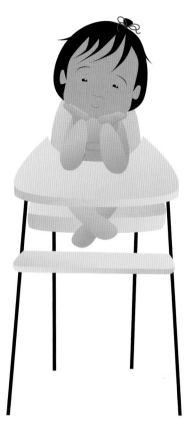

The family pooch can be a great motivator for your child, but if she isn't captivated by him, save the sign for when she is.

already signing?

You also might check to see if your child is already signing. Children can and will invent hand or finger gestures themselves or mimic actions that they have observed. Parents and other family members will also often teach signs without necessarily intending to bridge the communication gap. For example, many babies learn to wave "bye-bye" long before they are capable of saying it. This common action is really similar to sign language. And when you think about how cute a young baby is when she waves "bye-bye," just imagine how simply amazing it is to see a preverbal infant signing "more" at the dinner table or "all done" when she has finished eating.

nonverbal cues

Learning to focus in on your child's nonverbal cues is one of the keys to successful signing with your baby. Taking a moment to get down to your child's level on a daily basis is a really good way to hone in on her body language. Watching and interacting with her as she plays with her toys will give you plenty of opportunities for learning how her mind works.

motivating your baby

Waiting until the bowl is empty is the perfect time to ask if your child would like "more."

When you start signing with your baby, her daily routine can inspire many teaching moments for sign language. As well as using these occasions as they occur, you can also create wonderful opportunities for signing.

starting points

Mealtime is a logical starting point. When your baby is very small and ingests only breast milk or formula, a great deal of her attention revolves around food and its source. This is why a great majority of parents begin with a food or drink sign. "Milk" is very popular—with both parents and babies. As your baby grows, so does her repertoire of dinner options as well as signs. One unexpected benefit of signing I discovered is that your baby can sign while nursing. Lauren often did this. She would sign about what she was doing ("milk"), what she was hearing ("dog," "dad," or "brother"), what she was seeing ("baby"—an interesting one to experience while nursing), or what she wanted to do next, for example, "eat."

> "When you choose only a couple of signs to start with, you limit the number of contexts in which you are able to sign, lengthening the time it will take your child to sign back and develop an extensive vocabulary."

Dr. Michelle Anthony and Dr. Reyna Lindert,
Signing Smart with Babies and Toddlers:
A Parent's Strategy and Activity Guide

The tub provides plenty of signing moments—a favorite toy, such as a "duck," is a perfect example.

bath and bedtime

Bath time is another superb time with ample chances for learning. Take advantage of your baby's reaction to the temperature of the water and point out her rubber duck. You can also help your child communicate the concepts of clean and dirty.

Bedtime has lots of possibilities as well. Here you can talk about sleep, temperatures, and your child's preferred security items or bedtime companions as well as what you may see out of the window.

introducing opportunities

While allowing your child to explore her world on her own, you can certainly introduce your own signing opportunities as well. Don't be afraid of overwhelming your baby by showing her things she may be interested in.

signing at dinner

Food is such a great motivator. Signing will soon become commonplace around your dinner table as well as in restaurants when you brave an outing with your child. You not only have specific types of foods to sign about, but you will also have opportunities to describe the foods in terms of color and encourage the use of the sign for "more."

3 first signs

start talking

Are you ready to start talking? Great! This chapter will include a combination of both Need-Based Signs and High-Impact Signs. To get started, choose a small handful of signs from this chapter. It is important to remember that you need to speak the sign as you say it. Make sure you clearly enunciate the word that you sign. Think of signing as being an emphasis of what you say to your child instead of signing being an activity that is soundless.

getting vocal

Your child's signing will also not be soundless—he'll likely emphasize his signing vocally, as I discovered with my children. One time, I was trying to postpone a nursing session while shopping one day with 11-month-old Lauren. I got to witness some very loud punctuation to Lauren's requests—not only was she signing "milk" with both hands, right in my face, but she was also making very loud verbal protests and attracting a lot of attention. Needless to say, she got her milk.

Here are a few more helpful hints to guide you along your way:

BE HAPPY Frowning and bored voices will not make a baby eager to sign. Make it exciting.

BE FULL OF PRAISE Act excited when the baby uses a sign correctly, and let your baby know how wonderful you think he is.

BE VARIED Sign in different places. Don't just sign at home, for example, or when you have company, or when you're not in the public eye. Signing with your baby is most successful when it's worked into your life as a natural means of communication instead of something you do only part of the time or only in certain places.

BE PATIENT Babies can take weeks or even months before they make their first sign. And sometimes, even when they've done a sign correctly for a while, they may stop using it. Don't be discouraged if this happens. Keep on going and eventually they will get back on track.

"When you combine signs with words, you stimulate your child's auditory, visual, and kinesthetic senses. He hears the spoken word (auditory), observes your gestures and facial expressions (visual), and imitates your physical movements to produce a sign (kinesthetic)."

Laura Dyer, MCD, *Look Who's Talking!*

which hand do I use?

In sign language, the leading hand should be the dominant hand. If you are right handed, you will want to use your right hand to do all of the one-handed signs. For two-handed signs you will want to use your right hand to do most of the work while the left either stays still or acts as a foundation. The same applies to left-handed people, but in reverse. To avoid confusion, all of the signs in this book are illustrated with a right-handed signer, so be sure to remember to use the opposite hands if you are left-handed.

When baby wants his "milk" he will let you know—via sign as well as with vocalizations.

milk, eat, more

The most basic signs are the three presented here—"milk," "eat," and "more." I have spoken to many parents who made a successful start with these three signs. Use one, use all three, or choose a bigger handful with both Need-Based Signs (such as these three) and High-Impact Signs.

These signs are simple and generally easy for a child to pick up on, which is another reason parents choose them.

"Children are . . . likely to simplify the movements of signs, eliminate the movement completely, and/or make much more exaggerated motions than adults would."

Dr. Michelle Anthony and Dr. Reyna Lindert,
Signing Smart with Babies and Toddlers: A Parent's Strategy and Activity Guide

milk

Squeeze one or both hands, imitating a farmer milking a cow. Most people use one hand for an easier time, as often you will be holding your baby before he eats.

RECOMMENDED USAGE This sign is quite popular to begin with because drinking milk is usually one of your baby's favorite activities, and when he is young he does it quite often.

eat

This sign is sure to become one of your baby's favorites. Simply bring your fingers to your mouth as if you are holding a piece of food and are going to eat it.

RECOMMENDED USAGE This sign is great for mealtimes. Your baby will love being able to tell you he is hungry. This sign often persists well into toddlerhood—and even after he has mastered saying it.

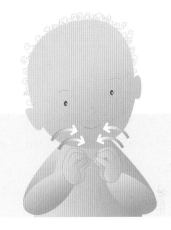

more

Bring the fingertips of both hands together in a repeated action.

RECOMMENDED USAGE This sign is probably one of the more popular signs babies like to do because it can be used not only for mealtimes but for virtually every facet of life, for example: Mommy, I would like "more" crackers, "more" swinging, "more" coloring, "more" petting the dog, "more" milk.

help, hot, hurt

These signs can be really good safety signs. They are valuable for interpreting your baby's needs and will help eliminate a lot of guesswork.

help

Your left hand "helps" to raise the right hand.

RECOMMENDED USAGE This sign is very important as your baby grows and begins to explore his surroundings. At many times, as a crawler, toddler, or preschooler, he will run into situations where he cannot make something happen, fetch a desired object, or be removed from a frightening situation. This will help him to get what he needs and will reduce the need to employ "20 Questions" to figure out the problem.

"It is important that your child sees you signing in various contexts, to allow him to understand the usefulness of signs in his world."

Dr. Michelle Anthony and Dr. Reyna Lindert,
Signing Smart with Babies and Toddlers: A Parent's Strategy and Activity Guide

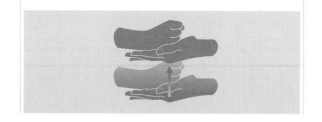

hot

Bring your hand to your mouth and then pull it away as if something were too hot to eat.

RECOMMENDED USAGE This sign is clearly very useful as a way to prevent your child from hurting himself. You can use it to show him to keep away from the stove or to wait before eating a bowl of hot food. It is also a sign that comes naturally for most mothers to teach as it can be used in everyday life.

hurt

Bring your two index fingers together in front of your body. Be sure to use a facial expression that shows you are in pain.

RECOMMENDED USAGE "Hurt" is one of the most effective signs that your baby will learn. It can eliminate a lot of guesswork and will enable you to assist your child so much faster. I also recommend that you use the sign over the body part in question. For example, you might sign "hurt" by your ear or over your child while asking, "Does your ear hurt?"

cold, drink, water

"Ah . . . a cold drink of water." As your baby gets older, you may want to model this sign sentence. For now, use each sign individually until your child shows signs of combining signs on his own (*see page 70*).

It is often good to start with signs that can be used in more than one situation, and these signs are great examples. If you use signs with various meanings, there are plenty of opportunities for repetition. It is easier to drive home the concept than if the situation only occurs once in a while.

cold

Hold fisted hands in front of your body while shaking your arms, such as you might do if you were cold.

RECOMMENDED USAGE There are many situations where signing "cold" will come in handy for both you and your child. You can use it to describe certain foods, and it can enforce the meaning of "hot" foods by comparison. As you run your child's bath, let him feel cool water while signing "cold." And of course, if and when it snows outside, "cold" is a fun sign to use when exploring winter.

drink

Bring your hand to your mouth as though bringing an imaginary cup to your lips.

RECOMMENDED USAGE This sign will help you teach your child to drink from a cup. Be it a sippy cup or a regular plastic cup, you can show your child his new cup as you sign "drink." Demonstrate drinking from a cup as you sign it, and then let him have a turn. Point out any other family members who are also drinking from cups.

water

Tap the side of your mouth with the letter "W" (*see page 105*).

RECOMMENDED USAGE This sign is easy to keep in mind because it uses the initial "W" to remind us of the word. You can use this sign for drinking water (later, perhaps, in combination with the sign for "drink"). When your child first starts to use a cup, water is a very good drink to begin with, for many reasons. You can also use this sign at bath time while teaching other relevant signs, such as "hot," "cold," and "bath."

dog, cat, bird

Family pets are an excellent starting point for signs—you may have noticed your baby gets very excited when he sees an animal. Animals make great High-Impact Signs, and babies love to have the tools to be able to communicate about them. Often a baby will not only be able to point out a pet to you as he notices it, but as he grows and his memory retains more information, he will want to discuss in signs what he remembers about his day, and his memories will often include pets.

dog

Pat your thigh as if you were calling a dog to "come here." You can follow this with a snap or you can choose to leave that step out. Both are valid ASL signs.

RECOMMENDED USAGE The sign is a natural motion for beckoning a dog to your side. Use it at home if you have a family dog. Sign "dog" saying, "Come here, Gus!" and to your baby, "Look! There is our dog." For pointing out dogs in the neighborhood or park, sign "dog" on the leg that is away from the animal. Make sure that your baby has noticed the dog first.

getting the sign right

A common approximation for "dog" that some children do (my daughter included) is patting the chest. Continue patting your thigh and he will eventually get it right—Lauren did.

cat

On one or both cheeks, brush imaginary whiskers.

RECOMMENDED USAGE As with "dog," you will want to use this when your child has noticed your family cat. You can also point out kitties in the neighborhood (one of Lauren's favorite pastimes is looking out of the front door for animals, as she is allergic to pets), or in picture board books.

bird

Use your thumb and forefinger (pointer finger) to form an opening and closing "beak."

RECOMMENDED USAGE Even if you don't have a pet bird, your child is likely to see birds out of the window, in your neighborhood, and at the park. Point out birds on the ground, in birdbaths, or in trees, and watch for him to notice birds in flight.

fish, bath, all done

These signs will help your little one discuss an animal, sign about bath time, and let you know in no uncertain terms that he is "all done"—hopefully without any screeching. At 22 months, my daughter Lauren found an interesting use of this last concept. She didn't like me to sing "You Are My Sunshine." The minute the first few words were out, she signed, "All done."

fish

The movement of the hand looks like a fish tail as it moves through water.

RECOMMENDED USAGE Not everyone has a pet fish, but you will come across fish in a pet store or in your favorite pond. To help your baby make the connection, you can sign "fish" in front of the tank to make sure he sees what you are doing, because chances are he will be enthralled by the fish.

"Signing while speaking allows you to have dialogue with your child much earlier than you could if you relied on speech alone."

Laura Dyer, MCD, *Look Who's Talking!*

bath

Scrub your chest with your two fists with thumbs up, as if you were washing yourself.

RECOMMENDED USAGE You should begin using this sign as you are filling up your baby's bathtub or the big bathtub. You can also use it to talk about a bird taking a bath or any animal frolicking in a puddle.

all done

Hold both palms facing upward, then flip to a downward position.

RECOMMENDED USAGE This is one of the most valuable signs you can teach your child. I suggest initializing its usage at dinnertime. You can sign "all done" as you clear your child's plate from his highchair, saying, "You are all done with your food." After he has grasped the concept, introduce it in other settings, such as playtime, bath time, or any other situation where being finished is the natural conclusion.

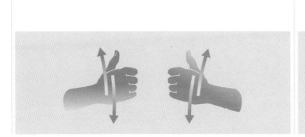

mother, father, flower

It is likely your baby will appreciate learning the signs for two of the most important people in his world—Mom and Dad. The great thing is that these signs can be used when Mom and Dad are right there or when they are just coming into the room. When your baby is older, he will likely show you which parent he would prefer to do something for him—maybe it's Mom who gives the best baths or Daddy who provides the best bedtime story.

mother

Tap the thumb of your open hand by the side of your chin.

RECOMMENDED USAGE Mom, Mother, Mommy, Mama . . . whatever you call her, your baby will appreciate having a sign for his mother. Mother herself can use this sign when talking about what she is going to do— "Mommy is going to change your diaper now," or, "Would you like to come with Mommy?" Other family members can make this sign as well when Mom comes into a room.

male and female signs

Generally, signs that refer to male people are made in the region of the forehead, and signs that refer to female people are made in the region of the chin.

father

Tap the thumb of your open hand by the side of your forehead.

RECOMMENDED USAGE This sign can be used in the same ways as "Mommy" can be used. Dad can use this sign when referring to himself as well as activities he is going to engage in with his baby, and Mom can talk about Dad when he comes in the room.

flower

Pretend you hold a blossom in your hand and move it from side to side in front of your nose as if you were smelling it.

RECOMMENDED USAGE If you plant flowers in your yard, bring your little one out on a warm day. Show him the flowers in your garden or in your flowerpots. Let him feel the petals and talk about how colorful they are. Point out blossoming bushes in the spring and enjoy a community planting together.

fan and light

fan

To sign "fan," simply rotate your index finger above your head, similar to the blades of a rotating ceiling fan.

RECOMMENDED USAGE Many babies will notice things on the ceiling, and they often become fascinated by ceiling fans. Take advantage of this fascination by introducing the sign for "fan." You might have to stand over your baby to get him to notice you. After your child learns this sign, he will appreciate the opportunity to tell you about the fan and even to request that it be turned on.

light

Flick the middle finger of your hand (from your thumb) lightly on the bottom of your chin a few times.

RECOMMENDED USAGE Again, light is a very fascinating topic for babies. He will notice lights everywhere—on the ceiling, his nursery lamp, at the grocery store, and even the traffic lights. Be sure to use the chances presented to you and introduce this sign at prime moments.

what's next?

At this point, you have learned twenty signs. Fantastic! You have the ability to pick and choose the signs you will teach your baby based on what he is interested in and what his needs are. You know the difference between Need-Based Signs and High-Impact Signs, and why it's important to offer some signs from each of those categories.

You have also learned a lot about what signing with babies is all about. Maybe you have also started signing with your baby and have realized how easy it really is. You have learned why I recommend using mostly ASL and why it isn't too difficult for babies to use. You have also learned how to motivate your baby and how to decide if the time is right for getting started.

Next, we will delve into more advanced topics. While signing may be easy to get started, the results may not be exactly as you expect, and some things may surprise you. You will also want to know how to establish a successful signing experience if your child is away from you—how will he be understood? Should daycare providers use signs so your child can keep up his skills? For troubleshooting and babysitters, read on. And there is a whole slew of new signs to learn.

signing with books

Picture board books are a great way to introduce signs for things you normally wouldn't come across. For example, even if your forays into neighborhood parks are few and you don't have the opportunity (or energy) to plant flowers of your own, you can choose a book that has pictures of beautiful blooms and teach the sign for flowers.

troubleshooting

overcoming obstacles

There may be a few obstacles on the way to signing success. Here are a couple of common ones and some ideas to help you to get around them.

skepticism

When someone you love doubts that your signing activities will be successful (or much worse, harmful to your child's development), it can be difficult to deal with. You might hear such discouraging statements as: "You're going to delay her speech." "What is the point?" "Are you teaching her to talk, too?" "You look ridiculous."

It may be worth your while to attempt to educate the other party on the benefits of signing, or you may want to wait until your child is signing back. All of my children converted a lot of people when they demonstrated the signs they knew. If someone is concerned about your child's future verbal development, please share the findings of studies of signing babies with them—i.e., that compared to nonsigners, signing babies score

higher in standard language and IQ assessments and show superior language production skills overall. Another suggestion is to involve the skeptical party with your signing activities. If the person becomes a part of your signing experience, he or she may become not only an active participant in your child's signing but even an advocate of signing as well.

saying "no"

Sometimes you might regret showing your child a certain sign, particularly if she requests it all day long, and especially if it is something that you do not desire her to have all day long. You might also hesitate to tell your baby "No." Many parents have worried that if they refuse a request it will discourage a baby to sign, but as Dr. Linda Acredolo explains this simply is not the case:

"Remember the old saying, 'Don't shoot the messenger'? Well, in the case where a baby keeps asking for cookies using a sign, the desire for the cookie is the message and the sign is just the

"I started signing with Laura from birth and she started signing back at seven months. It was a slow process, but well worth it. She did go through the stage where she would sign 'milk' for everything—but as her signs grew she stopped doing that. Laura signs about 25 words now. It has helped so much knowing what she wants—without the screaming!"

Paige, mother of Laura, 18 months

messenger. Fortunately, babies are pretty savvy about making the distinction. When a baby uses a sign to express a particular desire, she knows intuitively that her parent's answer will pertain to the meaning of her message, not to the symbol she used. She won't conclude that the parent is unhappy about the sign for cookie any more than a baby who says 'cookie' would think that refusing a cookie means general use of the word is bad."

"yelling" (signing with emphasis)

As your child learns signs, you may witness different variations of the signs depending on her mood or how badly she desires something. She may sign one-handed signs (such as "milk") with two hands or she may make vocal sounds as accompaniment. This is her way of saying, "Hey, look at me, I really need this!"

is this supposed to happen?

Sometimes the signing process doesn't seem to go as planned. What you will learn, however, is that sometimes what doesn't seem right is actually a natural milestone for learning to sign.

signing back

Parents are often worried that it will take weeks or even months for a baby to start signing. I always tell them that long before a baby starts signing, she will often make use of the signs in a different way—in other words, she may rely on and react to the signs that you, the parent, make but she hasn't quite got the ability to generate the signs herself.

Every baby develops at a different rate, and it can be hard not to compare your child to other children. Keep in mind, though, that many times a baby won't begin to sign back until she has passed her first birthday, even if her parents started signing when she was four months old. Many babies sign back by seven or eight months of age, but this can vary wildly, just like so many other physical and mental developments.

Another common event is that suddenly a baby who has previously signed suddenly stops signing completely. A typical reason is that she is concentrating very hard on accomplishing a

"Don't ask your children to sign out of context, perform for others, or compare your children to other children. Be careful not to show disappointment if your child chooses not to sign in a particular situation. Don't teach the signs, just sign. Let your baby discover."

Dr. Joseph Garcia, *Sign with Your Baby*

physical milestone and all of her resources are pouring into that as opposed to signing. Usually after this objective is mastered, she will go back to where she left off, especially if you haven't given up and have continued to sign correctly and consistently to her.

context is the key

Very often, a baby may produce several signs that look the same, particularly those that share a general likeness. A classic example would be any two-handed sign where the hands come together close to the midline of your body—such as

"more," "hurt," and "change." This can cause confusion on your part, but you need to keep in your mind that using context is an essential part of early signing. Your baby will, over time, be able to form the signs with greater accuracy and there will be less uncertainty.

Above all, maintain consistency on your side, and as your baby grows and matures her signs will become more precise.

is it a sign?

After you have made the decision to sign with your baby, you are probably pretty excited about the possibilities. So you begin with a few signs. Perhaps you've decided on "milk" for nursing, "eat" for when your baby is having a solid-food dinner, and "dog" because she loves your family pet so much.

A few weeks pass. You don't get discouraged because you know that it can take some time for your baby to make the connection between your movements and the activities and objects they represent. And soon, you realize that your child's hand motion starts to coincide with nursing.

one sign for everything

But wait. You now see her doing this motion when the dog comes into the room as well as when faced with a meal of enticing mashed banana. So you ask yourself (and your husband and mother also ask)—is she really signing at all?

The answer is: probably. When a child starts the signing process, she will often do any number of common things. One of the most common is to make the same sign for more than one thing or, in other cases, everything she sees.

If this is the case, then take heart, because your child has indeed made the connection between signs and what they represent. She may not be accurate right off the bat, but over time her aim and accuracy will indeed improve. Use context if you're not sure what sign she is making and always model the correct sign. In a short while she will grow more precise.

the daddy story

I started signing "Daddy" to my daughter but she took on other signs before starting this one. When she started signing it, however, I wasn't sure if she just thought it was a fun thing to do, because she wouldn't always do it when Dad was around. It didn't seem to be in context at all, and I had my doubts that she knew what she was doing with this one (even though she signed "milk" and "Cheerios" and other signs perfectly and properly).

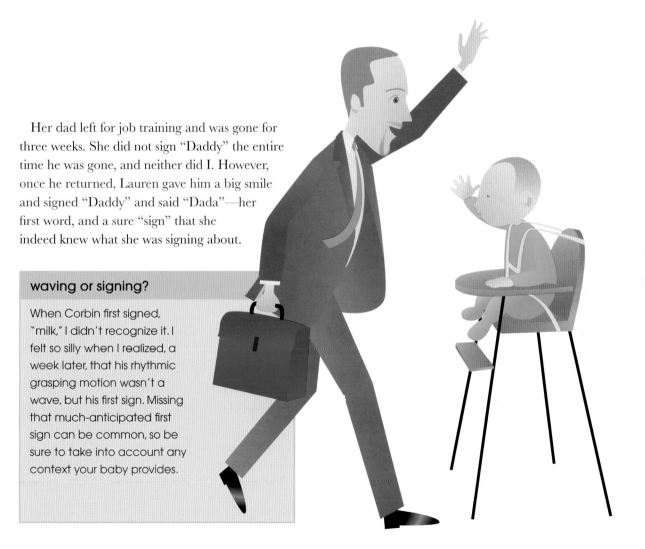

> "(Children's) early signs are likely to be larger and less controlled than yours (jabbing, clapping, hitting, as opposed to tight, small movements)."

Dr. Michelle Anthony and Dr. Reyna Lindert,
Signing Smart with Babies and Toddlers: A Parent's Strategy and Activity Guide

Her dad left for job training and was gone for three weeks. She did not sign "Daddy" the entire time he was gone, and neither did I. However, once he returned, Lauren gave him a big smile and signed "Daddy" and said "Dada"—her first word, and a sure "sign" that she indeed knew what she was signing about.

waving or signing?

When Corbin first signed, "milk," I didn't recognize it. I felt so silly when I realized, a week later, that his rhythmic grasping motion wasn't a wave, but his first sign. Missing that much-anticipated first sign can be common, so be sure to take into account any context your baby provides.

signing with caregivers

signing and the babysitter

Imagine this: you come to pick up your baby from daycare after a long day at work or after a quick run to the store. Expecting to find a delighted baby, you're greeted by your child's frustrated caregiver and your fussy infant. "What does this mean?" the babysitter asks, rotating her fists. You unhappily realize that your baby has been trying to ask for a changed diaper and his caregiver didn't understand the sign he was using.

involve your caregiver

Some parents who sign with their babies stay at home with their children while some work outside the home. Working presents an interesting situation because your baby likely goes to a babysitter for a certain amount of time during the day and he or she may not be aware that you sign with your baby. Even stay-at-home-moms can understand the problems that may arise when they leave their babies in the care of a grandmother or favorite aunt for a night out or a baby-free grocery-shopping event.

It can be a big concern for people who are trying to establish signing with their baby and are unsure of how daycare will affect their efforts, but I'm happy to report that children will usually sign well, even if their daycare providers do not sign, as long as there is consistency at home. Additional signing by your caregiver is icing on the cake.

Nevertheless, be upfront about signing with your baby with the sitter or daycare staff. Explain the benefits of signing with babies and show them how to do several signs. You may be surprised at their reaction—many centers and private daycares are incorporating baby signing into their regular routine and they may be adept at signing already.

"I only wish that more childcare professionals were knowledgeable about infant signing. I am the assistant director of a large childcare center. We use signs with our infants and have found that they teach each other."

Frankie, Assistant Director, Daycare Center, Bangor, Maine

When you show your sitter what signs your child is likely to use, it will help to eliminate future confusion and enable your child to be understood more easily.

maintaining consistency between home and away

Let your sitter know from the very beginning that you are signing with your baby. Make sure you demonstrate the signs your baby is likely to use.

Bring along a sign-language book or something similar that you can leave with the sitter each day for reference.

Let your sitter know which signs you're working on and tell her how to use them so your baby can learn new signs at the sitter's too.

Keep the lines of communication open between yourself and your child's caregiver and invite questions at every opportunity.

encouraging your caregiver

You may be surprised to find out that the daycare your child attends already uses sign language. If this is not the case, you might want to encourage your child's teachers, the director, or the caregiver to start signing with not only your child but other children as well.

highlighting the advantages

If your caregiver hasn't heard about signing with babies, she may show some initial skepticism or concern. You can explain the signing process to her, emphasizing the ease of the process as well as the benefits. She would probably enjoy having a quieter learning and playing environment as well as less frustrated babies and toddlers. It could also make the daily routines more predictable and happier for the children. If your child is already signing, that may be just the motivation that

your caregiver needs. There are few things more inspiring than seeing a baby who can sign.

The visual aspect of signing is also attractive to children, particularly in a group situation. It can be a great attention-getter and may lend some more depth to many group activities such as story time and art activities.

> "My son's daycare begins implementing sign language with the children in late infancy and early toddlerhood. The childcare providers find it very helpful, especially for the children who cannot yet clearly speak. It's also useful at home, and most of the signs that we use are ones I learned along with him."
>
> Erika, mother of Tavin, 29 months

for your caregiver

To start signing with your daycare charges, you will be following the same basic ground rules I have established in earlier chapters (start with "The Basics," *pages 18–19*.) There are several points to keep in mind:

• Make sure you have learned the sign well before showing it to your babies, toddlers, and children. You cannot do the sign one way and then the following day show them an altered version (or worse, show different versions to different children).

• Keep all of the staff up-to-date on which signs you are working on.

• Choose themes each week. Continue to show basic signs (i.e., "First Signs") but rotate through a set of five or so signs each week to keep things fun and interesting. For example, one week you might choose "farm animals," another week "foods," another week you might feature "at the zoo," and so on.

• Be sure to keep the parents up-to-date. Have book recommendations handy if you've encouraged a parent to sign with his or her child, and maybe even have a lending library of materials parents can check out.

using ASL

If your caregiver is going to begin a signing program at your facility, I recommend using an actual signed language, such as ASL. This way all of the babies and children will have a consistent learning environment and other parents can pick up on signs and sign with their children at home without confusing anyone.

signing with grandma

Involving family members in your signing activities can be a fun, exciting, and rewarding experience for everyone involved. As well as creating a blossoming signing environment for family get-togethers, you can lay a foundation for getting out of the house once in a while and avoid worrying about your family not being able to understand your child.

family gatherings

You may not have to make a concerted effort to introduce signing to your family. Chances are, you participate in family gatherings of some sort, be it family dinners, birthday parties, or holidays. If you are involved with the other members of your family, they are bound to notice your signing and may be really interested in it from the outset.

On the other hand, you might experience a little skepticism or disinterest from your parents or other family members. Many times they will be instantly converted when they realize the possibilities that signing presents (like Simon's grandma, *see* quote on opposite page), but other times you may have to show them some research on signing with babies to overcome it.

In either case, sharing your signing activities can be beneficial for your family and your baby. Show your parents or in-laws the signs you are working on, and use natural opportunities to reinforce the signs your baby knows and to teach new ones. See if you can get them involved in any way. Share your progress or, if you have just gotten started, explain how signing works and how they can help.

crossed wires

There can be some amusing misunderstandings during this learning process. One night my parents were babysitting when Corbin was 15 months old, and he was being naughty and standing on a chair. My dad said, "Corbin, get down!" and instead of getting down, he started signing "down." My parents didn't know what the sign was and the next day my mom said that Corbin was shaking his finger at my dad!

"Simon's grandma was very skeptical of my signing with Simon until she realized that he could tell her when he was hungry or thirsty. Suddenly, she wanted to know all the signs that he knew and started bragging about him to anyone that would listen."

Robin, mother of Simon, 12 months

If grandma signs too, your baby will benefit from having more than one person signing with her.

family support

Even if they do not actually teach your child new signs, just knowing what they mean can make a world of difference. My daughter Lauren was a proficient signer, and my mother and mother-in-law had to learn new signs almost every time we got together. My mom got a sign-language dictionary of her own and taught Lauren new signs when she was with her. We had a lot of family support for Lauren and Corbin because they were such adept signers—their aunts, uncles, great-aunts, great-grandmothers, and many other family members always wanted to know what signs the children were working on and would ask the meaning of new signs.

It's wonderful when a small child can look to and trust several adults to understand him, and it's helpful when he sees not only mom and dad signing. It can widen his vocabulary and give him more confidence that he will be understood.

6 developing signs

secondary words

In this chapter we will branch out a little and explore some objects, wants, needs, and conditions that you may run into on a daily basis with your child. They may be favorite things, first finger foods, exciting animals, and actions and instructions—all very handy to a blossoming signer and her parents. Also included are signs that lend themselves well to introducing concepts or that build on earlier signs.

"The building blocks of reading and writing are assembled long before a child enters school. From the moment a baby is born, he or she is constantly learning. It's a fact: children learn more in their first five years than during any other period of their lives. Because these years are so critical to your child's intellectual development, you, the parent or caregiver, play a vital role in influencing the growth of your child as a confident reader, writer, and lifelong learner."

www.reading.org

Visiting a zoo is exciting, motivating, and inspirational for your child, and "monkey" may prove to be a favorite animal—and sign.

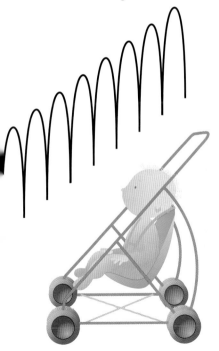

a developing awareness

As your baby grows, so will the world around her, and the ability to interact with that world will become very important to her. She will not only want to sign about things she can touch, but also the things that she sees across the room that she would like to view more closely or interact with.

make your own choices

Even though the title of this chapter is "Developing Signs," there still may be some signs here that you look through and decide to use when getting started. Think of these chapter divisions as suggestions and not what you must do to be a successful signing family.

book, car, boat

Here are a few of what might be your baby's favorite things. Of course, your baby may be interested in any number of other items, but these three were some of my children's favorites and still are—especially "book."

book

Hold palms together, then open them as if they are a book and you are opening it.

RECOMMENDED USAGE This sign can be used for only one thing—books—but what a powerful sign it is. Books are so important, and starting a reading habit very early can lead to a lifetime of reading as well as helping your baby's brain grow in all the right directions.

forming letter signs

Some signs ask that you form a particular letter sign, or use a certain letter hand (such as the "R" hand). Refer to the manual alphabet on pages 100–105 to learn how to make these.

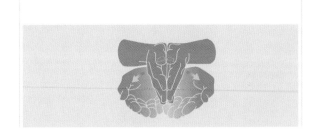

car

Mimic grasping a steering wheel with both hands and driving an imaginary car.

RECOMMENDED USAGE You can show your baby this sign as you look at a picture book with a car in it, when you bring out the toy cars, when you are going to get in your car, or as you see cars driving down the street. It can also be used with older toddlers as a safety sign, as in, "There is a car in the street. I'm going to carry you."

boat

Hold your hands together as if you were going to accept a handful of objects, and then move your hands forward (and together) as if they were a boat, gently bouncing on waves.

RECOMMENDED USAGE Unless you live in an area where you see real boats on a regular basis, this sign might be limited to toy boats, books, and/or television. It is still a captivating thing for your baby to see, however, so it may become one of her more important signs.

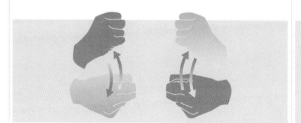

diaper, dirty, change

One thing your baby has been doing with great efficiency since birth is filling her diaper. You may be looking forward to the day when there are no more diaper changes—at least for this baby! One of the first ways parents get started with toilet learning is by introducing the three signs you see here. Once your child understands that a dirty diaper needs changing, you have planted the seeds for future potty training. Of course, it still may be years before she gets it, but teaching her the words to sign and then talk about it is a great start.

diaper

Bring the first two fingers of each hand together with the thumbs (a pinching motion) at the level of the waist—where you would fasten the tapes on a disposable diaper.

RECOMMENDED USAGE Use this sign to talk about the actual diaper. Sign "diaper" as you open a package of diapers or take a freshly laundered diaper out of the dryer. Show your baby the diaper before you put it on her.

dirty

Hold your hand under your chin and wiggle the fingers.

RECOMMENDED USAGE You will probably have a lot of opportunities to demonstrate this sign—at least if your child explores the world like my children do. You can use it before you wipe her face, saying, "Your face is dirty, and daddy is going to wipe it for you." You can use it when she gets a little too up close and personal with the dirt pile in the backyard. Last but definitely not least, you can use it when she has a dirty diaper.

change

Hold one fist on top of the other with bent index finger; change position.

RECOMMENDED USAGE This sign is great for illustrating a diaper change. If you suspect your child has a wet or dirty diaper, you can ask, "Do you need a change?" Also, sign "change" while placing her on the changing table or while changing her diaper. As she gets older, you can combine this sign with "diaper" and even "dirty" for a whole sign sentence.

cookie, cracker, bread

Favorite foods are really good signs to introduce. Food satisfies a basic need but it is also a very good motivator. Children are often really excited about food, and once they get past the milk-only diet and start foraging into baby food and then finger food, it is a very stimulating experience for them. Meal and snack times will provide many occasions to learn new signs and to reinforce them.

cookie

Rotate your dominant hand over your other hand (held flat) as if it were a cookie cutter.

RECOMMENDED USAGE Your child will really appreciate learning this sign—if she likes cookies, that is! You can use it for whatever you deem a "cookie" in your household. If you aren't planning to introduce real cookies for a while yet, you can use the "cookie" sign for a baby version, which may include home-baked treats sweetened with apple sauce or juice instead of refined sugars.

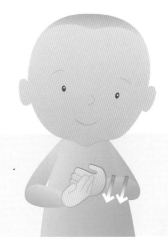

cracker

Tap the bent elbow of one arm a few times with the fist of your dominant hand.

RECOMMENDED USAGE The motion of this sign is fun for babies to imitate. Crackers are very popular with the nursery set and are often given to fussy babies in restaurants while their meal is being prepared.

bread

One hand is used to "slice" the loaf of bread signified by your other hand and held near your body.

RECOMMENDED USAGE Bread is also a very well-liked food for older babies and toddlers. Sometimes toasting the bread makes it easier for babies to eat it (in very small pieces, of course, and only for babies who are established "real" food eaters).

bear, cow, elephant

In addition to familiar family pets, your baby may be interested in learning signs for animals she might see on a farm or at the zoo. You can also find many animals in baby board books—either those specifically for sign language or otherwise. My daughter in particular couldn't get enough of animal signs.

gathering materials

You don't have to go out and spend a fortune on stuffed animals, videos, and books to inspire your child to sign about animals. Your local library should have enough materials to peruse and borrow. Some zoos have low admission prices or entrance is free. In addition, you might want to take a closer look at your baby's clothing—my three kids had ample clothing that featured one animal or another.

bear

Cross your arms in front of your body and "scratch" your upper arms.

RECOMMENDED USAGE This sign reminds me of a bear scratching on his tree. Bears are also quite popular with children. Many babies get teddy bears from a young age, and a bear may be a treasured security item. You can have fun combining signs with songs and rhymes about bears and other animals.

cow

Hold your "Y" hand *(see page 105)* to your temple and rotate forward with your wrist.

RECOMMENDED USAGE Children often love cows. Make use of any opportunity that you come across to show this sign to your child. She will probably not be able to create the sign perfectly at first, but as you know, give her time and continue modeling the correct sign. She will become more exact as she grows.

Approximations *(see box, page 64)* for many signs are often as cute as her first words will be, so you have that to look forward to.

elephant

Starting at your nose, "draw" the shape of an elephant's trunk.

RECOMMENDED USAGE This sign looks like one of the more fun aspects of an elephant— the trunk. Whether you spot these ponderous animals at the zoo or in a book, this will probably be a favorite sign in your house. Combine this sign with elephant sounds and walking motions and you have a great game to play while waiting at the doctor's office.

giraffe, horse, monkey

Exotic and exciting, these three signs will expand your child's vocabulary of animal signs. Learn them one at a time or all together, and they may be a big hit in your home.

A great way to introduce new animal signs is to imitate animal actions, or sounds. Ask your child to show you how a bunny moves or how a dog barks (all the while making the appropriate sign).

"Not only will they (animal signs) get your child's attention and allow him to participate with words/sounds/actions from a very young age, they'll also open the door to extended interactions and learning through play."

Dr. Michelle Anthony and Dr. Reyna Lindert, *Signing Smart with Babies and Toddlers: A Parent's Strategy and Activity Guide*

giraffe

Use your hand, starting at the area around your throat, and "draw" upward, showing the neck of a giraffe.

RECOMMENDED USAGE This sign visibly reminds me of the giraffe's long neck. Your child may reproduce it in any number of ways. My daughter would zing her hand up wildly above her head and then flap it around. Very endearing, and yes, she did ultimately sign it appropriately.

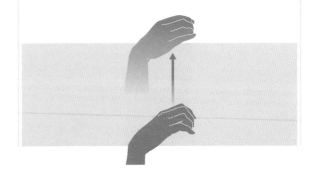

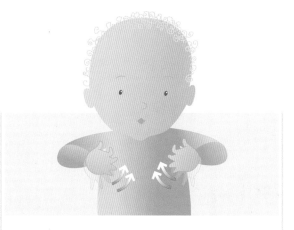

horse

The thumb of the right "H" hand (*see page 102*) touches the temple, while the two fingers move up and down a few times.

RECOMMENDED USAGE This sign will remind you of a horse's flicking ear. You can use this when you see a real horse—a very exciting experience for your child—or when your baby notices a toy rocking horse or wishes to play with his horse toy.

monkey

Bend your elbows to the sides, lift up your arms, and scratch your armpits with your fingers.

RECOMMENDED USAGE This is one of Corbin and Lauren's all-time favorite signs. When I introduced this sign, I added monkey noises (all while jumping up and down) and it became instantly popular and apparently hysterical. Monkeys are cute and funny and will be attractive to your child. This may be one sign that she picks up easily.

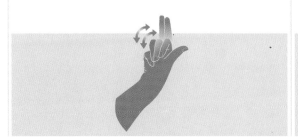

again, up, down

Empower your child! Giving her these three signs, which can be used as directives, will enable her not only to sign about her world but also to make things happen. These wants will be ones that your child expresses again and again and can be applied to many different situations.

again

Tap the palm of your nondominant hand with the fingers of your dominant hand.

RECOMMENDED USAGE For several reasons this sign is often confused with "more" and I recommend introducing it after "more" has been well established. Use it for any number of activities—reading a book, singing a song, dancing around the room, all the while asking, "Do you want to _____ again?" If you phrase the word correctly, your baby will soon attach the meaning to the word and the sign.

approximations

Approximations happen when your child doesn't quite yet have the ability to form the sign exactly. Each child will produce the sign in the best way that she can and eventually will be able to create the sign with greater precision. It's similar to how a child acquires speech.

up

Point your index finger up.

RECOMMENDED USAGE This sign can apply to the baby going "up"—for example, if she is fussing at your feet with arms extended, you might ask her, "Do you want up?" while signing the word. This is highly preferable to fussing, and it was one sign we used a lot during our signing years. This might also be introduced while your baby is in a swing.

down

Point your index finger down.

RECOMMENDED USAGE This sign is similar to "up" and can be used in much the same way— only the opposite. We got the most usage out of it when Lauren wanted out of her high chair. She would indicate that she wanted "down" and we would comply. When she was older, she would often combine it with "all done." How cool is that?

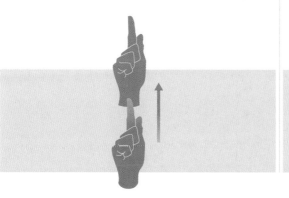

want, where, fall down

These signs can be for active signing learners who have mastered other signs and are expanding on those signs and concepts. They often work well when paired with other signs and multiple situations. However, you can introduce them to earlier signers as well (particularly "fall down").

want

Hold out both hands, palms up, and as you bring them close to your body, close them.

RECOMMENDED USAGE To remember this sign, think of grabbing something and then pulling it to you. You can show your child the sign in a "help" situation—for example, your child is trying to reach her favorite book that has fallen behind the couch. She may be signing "help" to you. Use this opportunity to sign "help" while asking, "Do you need help?" and introduce "want" by saying, "It looks like you want your book. Let me get it for you."

the shoe box

A shoe box (or even an empty cereal box) can provide a lot of opportunities to learn signs. You can teach and reinforce the concept of "where" and ask if your child "wants" what you have hidden in the box, in addition to teaching "out" and "in." Teach new vocabulary with different toys and soon your child will grasp not only new signs but new concepts as well.

where

Hold your index finger up and shake it back and forth, with a questioning look on your face (i.e., raised eyebrows, tilted head).

RECOMMENDED USAGE This sign can be used with "The Shoe Box" (*see box, page 66*) to teach this concept. And likely, once she learns it, your baby will use it often. Remember—facial expression can be very important when signing with your baby. Be sure to use your face when introducing and reinforcing this sign. It helps convey your meaning.

fall down

Your first two fingers first stand, and then fall down, on your other (flat) hand.

RECOMMENDED USAGE With this sign, it looks like a little person is standing on your hand. Uh oh! She fell down. Once children begin walking, they will often fall, either because they are still learning to keep their balance or because they are not watching where they step. Sometimes, though, if a child can sign about it, it may be less traumatic for her. This sign can easily be paired with "hurt."

out and into

out

Pull one hand "out" of the other one.

RECOMMENDED USAGE This sign can be used to illustrate the concept of "out" and may be utilized in a number of games with your child, such as "The Shoe Box" (*see box, page 66*). Used in conjunction with "in/into," your toddler will learn an interesting concept and will enjoy taking a favorite toy "out" and putting it back "in" again.

in (into)

This sign is the reverse of "out"—put your hand "into" another hand.

RECOMMENDED USAGE You can use this sign in the same ways as you use "out"—just in the other way. You may also employ the pair of opposites in other situations—such as putting her "into" a wagon, and when she is done (or has signed "all done"), showing her how to get "out."

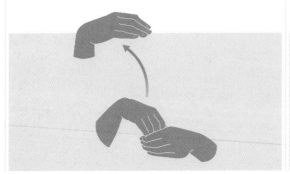

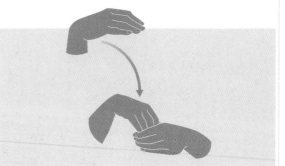

what's next?

You have learned a lot since the first chapter of this book. You probably have a better feel for what trouble spots to anticipate and how to work around them. You may be surprised that others have experienced what you are experiencing, but be assured that you are never the only one. You have also learned a lot about establishing a successful signing relationship with your child even if she is away from you at some point— whether it be a short babysitting stint at a relative's or in formal daycare.

Next, you will learn how signing functions with older children and how you can continue signing with your child even as she careens headlong into her preschool years—and beyond. You will find out how signing can help with—but not eliminate—temper tantrums as well as how to branch out and meet other signing parents, and even form your own signing groups. Also, look forward to learning the manual alphabet and colors—as well as activities to incorporate these into your child's early education.

Ready, set, go! You and your baby are now geared up to learn more signs, concepts, and activities.

sign combinations and sentences

combining signs

If you sign with your baby long enough, or if he continues to sign well into toddlerhood, you may begin to experience some really interesting sign combinations from your child. I'll never forget the time when Corbin, then a toddler, first saw snowfall. Gazing out of the window, he was eager to tell me, by signing "white" and then "rain," about the "white rain."

natural progression

Just as children naturally begin to combine spoken words, they too will begin to combine signs. This may begin as early as 12 months but may be more likely to occur closer to their second birthday. It represents a natural step in language acquisition (most children combine at least two words by 24 months). Since signing can often mirror this process, it's reasonable to expect children to use two signs together. Don't be concerned that your child will combine signs and fail to combine words; his signing developments will reinforce his verbal development and vice versa.

Combining signs allows a child to further expand on his ability to communicate effectively. The first time your child does this, it may surprise and astound you, and as his vocabulary grows so will his confidence, and so too will the number of sign sentences he displays.

eliminating guesswork

Combining signs helps your child to expand on what he wants and needs. It is a level of communication that is beneficial to you both as it helps to narrow down the options. There will be less guesswork on your part if your child wants something that might be one thing or it might be another—for example, if your child wants his stuffed kitty toy, but there are two, he might be able to differentiate from the outset that he would like the green one rather than the white one.

The progress your child makes doesn't stop at combining two signs, either. Children can and will combine three, four, and five signs together if they have the vocabulary and the desire!

the five-sign sentence

One day when my daughter was two years old, she was playing with her wind-up bunny. She enjoyed causing it to fall off a small table, and one time when it did so, she looked at me, delighted, and signed "bunny fall down mommy black shoe." Indeed, when I investigated, I found her bunny resting in my black shoe where it had fallen.

"combiners"

The advanced signer can combine many different kinds of signs to get his point across. Some of the more common combinations to look for would include:

"more" + another sign

"again" + another sign

color + object

person or object + "go"

object + "mine"

"up" + another sign

"down" + another sign

combining signs and speech

In addition to combining two or more signs together, there will likely be a time when your child will put together both signs and words in the same sentence.

bridging the gap

Most children begin speaking before they are done signing. Using sign language with babies is, as you will discover, a perfect bridge for the communication gap that occurs before they are capable of verbal speech. It really isn't surprising that children can and will combine signs and spoken words. This can come about at any time after your child says his first word.

As children move from signs to words, they may pick up on spoken words quickly but may continue using signs to fill gaps in their vocabulary. Children who can sign will very often pick up spoken words at a fast pace, simply because they are already acquainted with the object, action word, or concept, and it becomes simply a matter of testing the word with their more mature verbal muscles.

You also might notice your child continues to use a sign for a word that he can say. This may be out of habit—and what a great habit it is—or it may be a little trick he uses to get your attention. Since we, as parents or caregivers, tend to make a great

from signs to speech

Signs gradually do give way to words. Your once actively signing baby will soon begin to replace each sign with a word, and once speech begins, you will find that it doesn't take long to do, simply because your child already knows what most things are due to signing. The most frequent signs your child uses will likely be the last to go. Also, continue to look for the signs that usually get your child what she wants. My son held on to the "please" sign well after he could say the word simply because I found it difficult to say no to such a sweet little boy using such a nice sign so politely—and he knew it.

"It is wonderful to be able to 'talk' to my child at a young age. We truly believe that the signing is why she talks so well now. When she started speaking it was in multiple words and she used her signs and words together so that we can understand her."

Jo Di, mother of Savannah, 12 months

fuss and pay attention when our baby signs to us, they pick up on this nuance and continue to use it to their advantage. Emphasis is also a motivation to using signs at the same time as spoken words. Babies commonly use two hands to emphasize one-handed signs (such as "eat") and a toddler will often sign a word as he says it to make sure you know that he really means it.

word rush

You can look forward to some really interesting conversations as your child signs and speaks at the same time. As you are running errands or dining out, people may really notice your little signer/speaker even more than they did when he just signed. Enjoy this special time because it may not last long. Many children, when they begin to speak, learn to say a lot of words in a very small amount of time.

bridging the gap

You have a unique opportunity to be a really good signing model for your child. With just a single sentence you can teach multiple signs as well as encourage your child to create sign sentences of his own.

telegraphic speech

Often when children begin speaking they use a particular speech pattern that is known as "telegraphic speech." When you think about what is written in a telegram, only the most important words are used—nouns, verbs, and some adjectives. Even though you speak in complete sentences and need to also model complete sentences for your child, keep the telegraphic speech pattern in mind when choosing words to sign (or emphasize) as you speak.

"Although your baby won't have any idea about the formal rules of grammar until he's well into his school years, he'll be learning language by hearing the speech of people around him—especially you."

Robert E. Owens, Jr., Ph.D., *Help Your Baby Talk*

When signing to your child, choose important words to focus on. When you first started signing with your baby, you generally focused on a single word, but as your child grows and his ability to comprehend expands, you can use several signs in each sentence if you would like to.

An earlier example might be: "Look at your 'bear.' He is going up high!" You would sign "bear" in this sentence. A more advanced signer might enjoy signing: "Look at your 'bear.' He is going 'up' high!" In this sentence, you would sign "bear" as well as "up."

expanding vocabulary

You can focus on expanding your child's vocabulary this way. If you sign more than one word in a conversation with a toddler, he may be able to pick up more signs this way. You can beef up your signing vocabulary each week and immerse your child in signs. If you sense he is getting overwhelmed, you can cut back the amount of signing you do, but as with any

choosing key words

Good focus words are nouns, verbs, and adjectives. Keep your child's interests and desires in mind as well when picking key words. Establish a basic vocabulary list and stick with those words when you sign.

language, the more you sign with your child the more signs he will eventually know.

You also might be interested in helping him work out how to combine signs on his own. Children also learn from watching you interact and speak or sign with others. Try using more complicated signing sentences when you speak with your spouse and friends as well as when you are interacting with your child.

8 taming tantrums

signs of stress

One of the most touted benefits of signing with babies is that when children have the ability to sign they can avoid large-scale emotional flare-ups, also known as temper tantrums. How does this work exactly?

asking for help

You look up and see your toddler is in distress. She notices you are looking at her and earnestly signs "help" a couple of times. You sign back "help" while asking, "What do you need help with?" She points to the ceiling and makes an attempt at signing the word "balloon" that you recently began to show her (you got lots of practice at a recent party). You retrieve the balloon, hand it back to your child, and all is well—except when she loses her grasp yet again, and the classic toddler game of fetch-and-retrieve starts all over. "Help" is one of the more useful, or should I say helpful, signs as far as signing with babies goes. It provides both children and parents with an invaluable communication tool.

keeping control

Babies and toddlers very often find themselves stuck in one predicament or another, and if they don't talk, they have little hope of rescue. They are often newly mobile in a world over which they have little power and have a desire to do things they frequently cannot physically accomplish. For example, they need help opening a container of blocks, or help scooping up their macaroni with a spoon, or help recovering their favorite toy from behind the couch, or help manipulating the drawbridge on their play castle. The frustration a child feels in a situation where she has little or no control is overwhelming and often results in tears or in a full-out tantrum. This of course results in stress and frustration on the part of the parent, who may often feel helpless and perhaps irritated at the situation.

The use of sign language, then, can help prevent tantrums or stress before they begin because your child has the tool she needs to communicate the exact nature of her wants, fears, desires, or needs.

"If I could only teach Simon three signs, they would be 'milk,' 'more,' and 'all done.' While 'milk' and 'more' might be obviously helpful, Simon's ability to tell me when he is all done with something (sometimes before he even starts!) has, I am quite certain, averted many a tantrum."

Robin, mother of Simon, 12 months

not a cure-all

Signing does help prevent tantrums, but it is important to note that it will not completely eliminate a toddler's frustrations and tantrums, and with some children it won't be readily apparent that it is helping at all. It can be hard to quantify results when you're not sure how your child would have reacted without signing, so keep your spirits up and know that you are giving your child an awesome communication tool that likely is easing her frustrations.

key signs

Every parent will find signs that prove to be the most useful to them and to their children, but there are three in particular that I feel are so helpful and important that—even though they are covered elsewhere in the book—I want to highlight them again. Throughout my signing experiences with my own children as well as talking with other signing parents, I wanted to emphasize these extremely useful signs and I hope that you will add them to your child's sign language vocabulary.

There are other signs, of course, that you will find useful in your home. These three, however, are special. They can really boost a child's ability to get around the many hurdles she has to face on a daily basis and can also give her a sense of control of her world.

help

"Help" gets results fast. When you are small, life can be frustrating because you cannot physically accomplish everything you would like to do. Babies can sign "help" in so many different situations and its use is incredibly effective. *See page 28.*

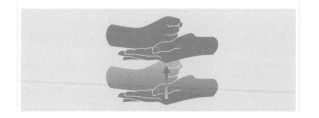

all done

Teaching your child the sign for "all done" is giving her an opportunity to voice a very important opinion about her activities. Before your baby can talk she will likely find herself in situations that she would prefer not to take part in—or would like to finish—and this sign, if it is heeded, can help prevent a full-scale meltdown. *See page 35.*

please

Teaching your child to sign "please" will help her to be polite, but it has an added benefit to your child. She may use the sign to let you know that she really would like to have or do something and this will allow you to weigh your decision with that in mind. I don't advocate giving in to your child each time she signs "please" but it will help you pay attention to her wants and needs. *See page 98.*

a new arrival

Signing can be a beautiful connection between you, your child, and a new arrival—your newborn baby.

averting frustration

Your child may become frustrated toward the end of your pregnancy if your activity level declines and you aren't able to play and interact with her as much as you used to. This could cause some tantrum-like behavior that you may be able to alleviate with signing as discussed earlier. Enlist the help of family members now, before the birth, and make sure that they can help you out when your baby arrives. My mother-in-law took Dagan to a carousel for the afternoon when Corbin was a newborn and it was an act of kindness I will never forget. Be sure the family member is familiar with your child's signing.

As the baby grows older signing can be a really fun way to connect with both of your children. If you decide to sign with your new baby it is likely your older child will have a lot of fun helping you out. If your older child is still signing she will enjoy watching the baby learn, and if she is old enough to have dropped some signs, she will likely be able to pick up signing again quite easily.

sibling bonding

Signing can be a special bond between the siblings. Dagan taught Corbin signs that he refused to learn from me and Corbin taught Lauren even more signs that he remembered from his babyhood. Teaching a younger sibling signs is an excellent self-esteem booster. Your older child will be proud, and your baby will be excited to be able to communicate with her brother. Another interesting thing to look for is when signing becomes a "secret language" between siblings. The ability to communicate without speaking a word can be very appealing to your children—but maybe not to you if they are planning devious activities!

"Children often lose their ability to communicate when frustration or fear mounts, or when coming to a full-fledged tantrum. Invite your child to sign instead of trying to get her to talk about it. You might be surprised at what your child can communicate with signs when words won't come."

Dr. Michelle Anthony and Dr. Reyna Lindert, *Signing Smart with Babies and Toddlers: A Parent's Strategy and Activity Guide*

the first connection

Many young toddlers aren't able to visualize an actual baby inside their mother's tummy, so their first meeting after the birth may be a really exciting event. Watch your older child carefully to see what signs she shares as she takes in her new sibling, and encourage her by signing too.

Baby wants milk. Your toddler may become a member of the "milk police" by informing you when her sibling wants to nurse.

going beyond "milk" and "mommy"

Your child has possibly mastered the signs that I have shared with you so far, or maybe you are looking for more advanced signs for an older child, or your particular toddler isn't interested in some of the first signs. The signs contained in this chapter will expand on what your child has learned as well as introducing new concepts that will appeal to an older toddler and preschooler (and beyond).

games and activities
You will learn ways to make some signs into a game and how to incorporate the alphabet and colors into your learning activities At this stage in your child's development, you can also teach him to count.

Expanding your child's signing vocabulary can help her sign "cake" at her next party.

Playtime can lead to opportunities for showing and learning advanced signs.

at what age should I show the ABCs?

You can start showing your child the ABCs whenever you like, but he may not pay much attention until he is 18 months or two years old—or even later than that. To get started, sing the ABC song while showing your child the signs. The first letters your child may recognize may be those in his first name. Write it out for him and speak and sign each letter. Point out letters in his books while clearly saying the letter and showing him the sign for it.

Don't force the learning, however. As with everything else, keep up with your child and also go beyond his current level, but if he isn't interested, try again another day.

sign and speak

Signing can continue well after your child learns to speak. It can also help him to explore objects and concepts that he may not be able to verbalize yet. You have also learned that signing can continue to help reduce frustration because he either cannot say what he needs or because he is unable physically to accomplish something. I noticed that signing helped Corbin show empathy at an early age. I got a bad scratch on my leg when he was a toddler, and weeks after it healed he continued to sign "hurt" after pointing to my leg. It can also be a really fun addition to your child's daily routine and a game, as well as a communication tool.

how about colors?

Colors can be lots of fun to learn. This is something you might start introducing at around two years of age or later. Begin by pointing out basic colors. Start with primary colors (red, yellow, and blue) and then introduce secondary colors (purple, orange, and green) before moving on to black, white, brown, and pink.

grandmother, grandfather, family

Your child may want to learn the signs for her grandparents— especially if they have a great importance in her life. Learning labels for family members is an important first step. Later you may want to differentiate between grandmas (my mother-in-law is "Apple Grandma" because she always brings Lauren a fresh apple when she visits), but for starters you can begin with the basic signs.

approximation for grandparents

A common approximation for "grandmother" or "grandfather" is multiple bouncing instead of a double bounce. If you see your child wildly bouncing his hand around the chin or forehead area and you're not quite sure what he means, consider his grandparents as the source.

grandmother

This sign is similar to "mother" except instead of tapping your chin, start at the chin area and bounce it away from your face two times.

RECOMMENDED USAGE: Use this sign to refer to your child's grandmother—you can use it in her presence, as you approach her house, and as you talk about her. As with "mother" and "father," your child's grandma might use the sign to refer to herself as she interacts with her grandchild. If your child has a special gift or treat from grandma, be sure to let him know that it came from her by using the sign.

grandfather

As with "grandmother," this sign is comparable to "father." Instead of tapping your temple area, start at the temple (or forehead) area and bounce it away from your face two times.

RECOMMENDED USAGE: Grandpa can be a fun guy and your child may be quite enthusiastic to learn this sign. Always pair the sign with the spoken word, and be sure that your child knows you are talking about his grandfather rather than another relative who happens to be in the same room.

family

Hold both "F" hands *(see page 101)* together at the thumb and index finger and move them away from your body in a circular motion until the hands meet again on the pinky side.

RECOMMENDED USAGE: This sign is perfect for family get-togethers. Tell your child, "This is your family," while making the sign.

brush teeth, play, outside

These signs deal with some of your child's daily activities. Routines are very important to your child. They let him know what to expect on a daily basis and are a way to keep him "in the know" as you go about your lives.

brush teeth

Use your index finger as if it were a toothbrush, moving it up and down in front of your teeth.

RECOMMENDED USAGE: This sign is easy to remember because it looks like what it represents. My children all loved brushing their teeth and appreciated learning the sign. Lauren, at age three, will go in the bathroom and brush her teeth for fun at all hours of the day, but we still utilize the nighttime brushing as part of her bedtime routine.

number of signs

Parents often wonder how many signs to introduce to their child when they start signing. I recommend that you start with six or even more, as evidenced by the Signing Smart program developed by Dr. Michelle Anthony and Dr. Reyna Lindert (*see page 13*).

play

Form a "Y" *(see page 105)* with both hands and rotate your hands at the wrist.

RECOMMENDED USAGE: When you ask your child if he wants to play, be sure to show him this sign. The concept might be a little abstract for younger children, but as your child grows so will his comprehension and he will make the connection with the sign and having fun.

outside

At shoulder level, grasp the air in front of your body and pull it away.

RECOMMENDED USAGE: Some parents choose to use the sign for "out" for this concept *(see page 68)*, but others prefer to use this ASL sign for "outside." Use it when your child is simply gazing outdoors or when he clearly would like to go out and play. In the warmer months this may be a sign that he uses a lot. You might like to combine this sign with the one for "play."

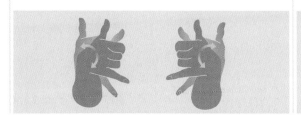

apple, grapes, candy

Here are some more fun food signs for you and your child to learn. Although you will most likely not be introducing these items into your child's diet until he is three or older (particularly raw fruits or vegetables) because of the choking hazard, you can learn the signs earlier as you look at books or flash cards that depict these items, or as you shop. As with most food signs, your child might really enjoy learning these signs because they will allow him to communicate with you about his favorite foods.

apple

Twist your bent index finger, or "X" hand *(see page 105)* on your cheek.

RECOMMENDED USAGE: This sign reminds me of twisting the stem out of an apple before eating it. Apples are one of the more easily recognizable fruits. Point them out as you go grocery shopping and later, when your child has learned some colors, combine the color of the apple with the sign for the apple itself. Often children will group many fruits and vegetables together and label them all apples. Lauren often called grapes "little apples."

grapes

Tap your spread-out fingers along the back of your base hand while moving them down toward the fingers.

RECOMMENDED USAGE: The movement and the shape of your hand resemble a cluster of grapes. Children enjoy the flavor and texture of many kinds of fruits and grapes are no exception. They also come in several colors, giving you another opportunity to combine signs for the object and its color. Grapes are a big choking hazard so when you do introduce the actual fruit, cut it into small pieces.

candy

This sign is similar to "apple" except you use your index finger straightened near the corner of your mouth.

RECOMMENDED USAGE: I don't recommend children consume candy, but I am grounded in reality and I know that children really enjoy sweet treats. I have included the candy sign on the same page as "apple" for comparison purposes, but be aware that your child may produce exactly the same sign for both of them even though the meanings are quite different.

ice cream, cake, party

Birthday celebrations are occasions to introduce even more exciting signs to your child. You can take full advantage of the festivities to initiate new signs that may not be part of your everyday schedule. Even if your little one isn't the birthday boy, he will be excited to attend and benefit from the social activity of the party as well as the fun new foods to try.

Of course, not all young children are outgoing social animals (my two younger children included) and it was a great benefit for them to learn the signs so they could be prepared for the experience before being enveloped by it. Even though they would cling to me from an early age, they still loved to sign about what they had experienced.

ice cream

Hold your closed fist in front of your mouth and move it back and forth as if it is the cone and you are licking it.

RECOMMENDED USAGE: You can choose to stick your tongue out as well when demonstrating this sign—it is correct either way. Your child might be a little put off by the temperature of this frozen treat, which is an opportunity to not only sign "ice cream" but to enforce the usage of "cold" as well.

cake

Slide your "C" hand *(see page 101)* over your other palm.

RECOMMENDED USAGE: This sign reminds me of slicing a piece of cake. It is perfect for baby's first foray into cake eating as well as the many times thereafter when he will partake of cakey goodness. Watching a baby experiment with his first plateful of cake is almost as much fun as eating it yourself, and it has loads of signing opportunities as well—including "cake," "eat," "dirty," and then "clean."

party

This sign is similar to "play" except that instead of rotating the "P" hands *(see page 103)* they swing from side to side.

RECOMMENDED USAGE: The movement of your hands may remind you of people dancing at a party. Use it when guests start arriving or when you are going to someone else's party. An older child may remember the party and use the sign when thinking about it or wanting to share his experiences.

lion, tiger, duck

Your child may well be an animal lover, so here are a few more animal signs for him to learn. Sometimes children get confused with animals that look the same or are the same general type of animal (such as lion and tiger, or duck and bird), but as always, maintain consistency and wait for your child to arrange animals into their proper group when he is ready to do so.

lion

Run your hand from the front to the back of your head, over your imaginary lion's mane.

RECOMMENDED USAGE: Couple this sign with an angry roar and you may have one fascinated child. Big cats are very well liked by young children and are an exciting attraction at the zoo as well as in your child's stuffed animal collection.

remembering animal signs

Animal signs are often really easy to remember because they look like what they represent. Although not all ASL is like this, signs that resemble what they represent are quite a bit easier for us parents and caregivers to remember, which comes in especially handy once your child goes through a period of rapid learning.

tiger

Draw "stripes" with both hands along either side of the face.

RECOMMENDED USAGE: This sign visibly resembles the stripes on a tiger's face. Be sure to note the tiger's stripes and colors. You don't have to sign "black," "orange," or "white" at first, but if you point the colors out it may be easier for your child to tell a tiger from a lion.

duck

Create a "beak" with your first two fingers along with your thumb; hold to your mouth in the "beak" position.

RECOMMENDED USAGE: This sign resembles the sign for "bird" but you can help your child tell the two apart by making the proper animal noises along with the corresponding sign. A common approximation of "duck" involves the entire hand forming the beak instead of two fingers and a thumb. This also can happen with the sign for "bird."

off, on, home

"Off" and "on" can be applied to many situations while the "home" sign has just one meaning.

There are benefits to both types of signs. When you can apply one sign to multiple instances, you explore the word thoroughly and are able to share a concept with your child that will allow him to see it used in different contexts. It also gives you ample opportunity to practice the sign, which will assist your child with his comprehension and will aid your comfort level and ability to remember how the sign is made.

Signs that have just a few uses or a single use are often really motivating—the desire to learn and communicate with them can be quite high. Several High-Impact Signs are like this.

on

Simply place one flattened hand on top of your base (also flattened) hand.

RECOMMENDED USAGE: This sign can be applied to many situations. "On" can be used to describe the position of your child's favorite objects, people, or toys. Is his doggie "on" the couch? Is his teddy "on" the kitchen table? Does he want to be "on" the chair?

off

Start in the "on" sign position, and then move up and off of your base hand.

RECOMMENDED USAGE: The most obvious use of this sign is as the opposite of "on." Lauren used this sign in a really interesting way. She has several books that have small ladybugs on the pages. She would try to pick the bugs off while signing "off"—it was a great joke to her.

home

The "O" hand shape *(see page 103)* moves from the side of your mouth to your cheek.

RECOMMENDED USAGE: This sign may remind you of two things you do most often at home—eat and sleep. Use it when you are out and ready to head home, and sign it as you arrive home. Soon your child will make the connection and may request to go "home" when he is worn out, tired, or cranky.

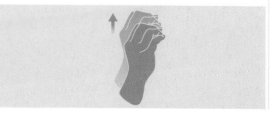

shoes, socks, tree

The signs on these pages will come in handy during your daily routine and for some nice neighborhood investigations. Get your child's shoes and socks on—it's time to go to the park and learn about nature.

shoes

Tap both "S" hands *(see page 104)* together on the thumb side.

RECOMMENDED USAGE: Think of shoe heels clicking together when you make this sign. Babies and toddlers often love this one because they are fascinated by shoes, and since your child may wear them on a daily basis, the sign can be really easy to learn. It is, however, one sign that may confuse you when your child signs it, since it involves bringing both hands together (similar to "more" but with the hands fisted and pointing to the ground).

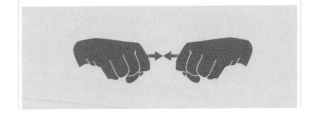

change your scenery

It's a good idea to introduce your child to signs in new situations—even when reinforcing the same "old" signs. A change of your surroundings can keep your days bright and fascinating and can generate more enthusiasm from your child.

socks

Slide both index fingers together while pointing down.

RECOMMENDED USAGE: Show your child this sign before you put his socks on. For a fun way to encourage the sign—if you aren't particular about his socks matching his clothes—allow him to choose a pair to wear. As well as being fun, it can help him learn the sign.

tree

Hold your right elbow on the back of your left hand while your right hand, fingers splayed, turns back and forth.

RECOMMENDED USAGE: The fingers of your right hand represent the branches of a tree. Point out trees in your yard or at the park, or as you explore your neighborhood. Get up close to discover the different textures and colors—especially fun during the fall season.

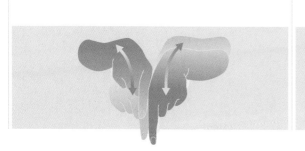

please, thank you, me/mine

A polite child is a wonderful thing to behold, and it can be especially cute if the child knows a few polite signs. Many children will hold on to these particular signs well after they have the ability to say the words—whether it is for emphasis or because they know how adorable they look, I'm not sure—but some parents (myself included) find themselves giving in more readily when their child requests something accompanied by a big-eyed "please."

please

Your flat hand makes circles on your chest.

RECOMMENDED USAGE: As your child enters toddlerhood, introduce this sign when you can see that your child desires something in earnest. Don't require your child to sign "please" before you give him what he requests, but encourage use of the sign and use it yourself when, for example, you ask him to hand you something.

blowing kisses?

I'll never forget Corbin trick-or-treating for the first time at age two. Not only did everyone think he was a girl but they assumed he was blowing kisses instead of politely signing "thank you."

thank you

Your flattened hand will start on your chin and extend out and down in an arc.

RECOMMENDED USAGE: When your child signs this to you, you might think at first he is blowing kisses. In fact, other people will often mistake this sign for that particular gesture. This sign is also a great one for you yourself to demonstrate, and demonstrate often. Sign "thank you" after he hands you something, or puts away a toy, or behaves gently with his younger sister or a neighbor's dog.

me/mine

When signing "me," point to your chest. When signing "mine," pat your chest with your flattened hand.

RECOMMENDED USAGE: These two signs are not interchangeable or necessarily polite, but they can both be really important to your child as he examines his world and determines what is his (or what he would like to have). Learning these signs might help eliminate some hollering from your child, unless of course what he deems as "mine" is not his at all!

letters: a through f

Some signs require the use of a particular hand shape in order to form it correctly. The following pages will show you the manual ASL alphabet. Learning the signs for the alphabet will help you sign appropriately, it will come in handy, and is fun, too.

Learning letters can start as early as age two and can be particularly enjoyable when combined with the signs for the alphabet as well as the alphabet song. A very good place to begin would be pointing out the letters in your child's name. Write your child's name in capital letters and name each one while signing each letter.

the alphabet song

If your child isn't interested in this activity (which he may not be until he is older), you might try introducing the alphabet song. I recommend running through it a few times yourself until the manual alphabet becomes more natural to you, and then sharing it with your child. He may not be able to reproduce any of the letter signs right away, but chances are, he will love the song and may think of the signing as a game.

forming the letters

Your child may have some difficulty forming the letters exactly as they should be shaped. I suggest you physically help your child form the letters, but only if he lets you. If he does not, you can adopt a "wait and see" approach, because as you have learned previously, children will grow more precise as they mature and practice their signs.

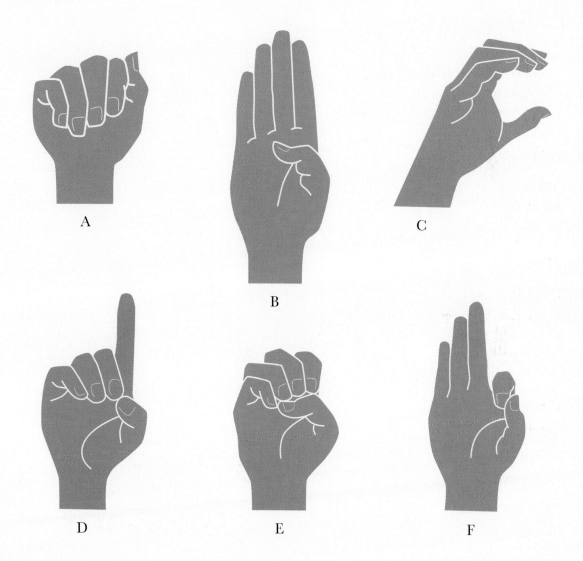

A

B

C

D

E

F

letters: g through q

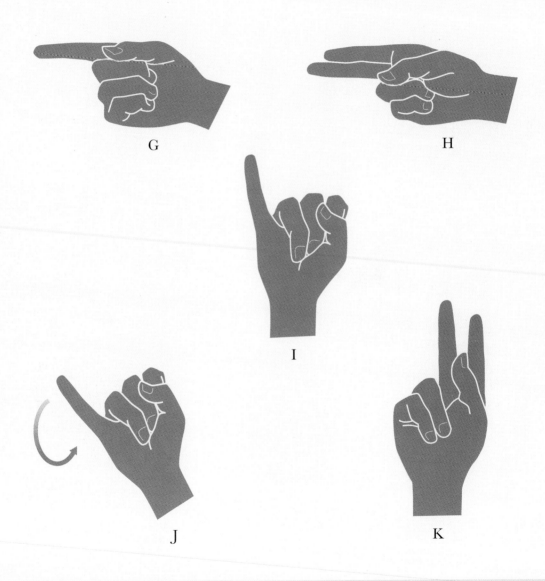

G

H

I

J

K

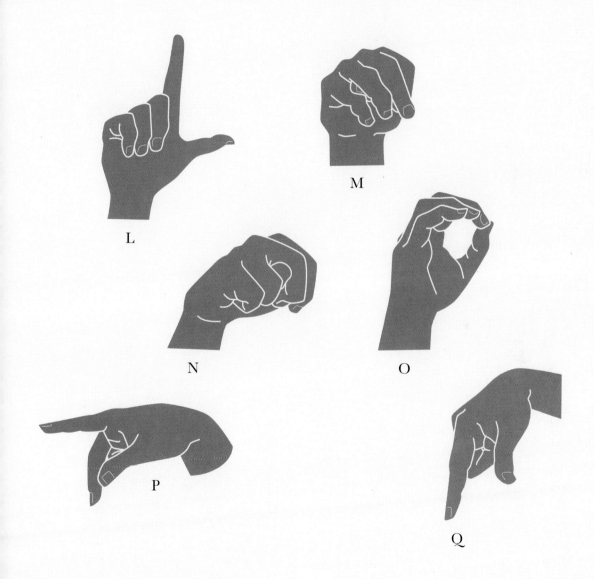

L

M

N

O

P

Q

letters: r through z

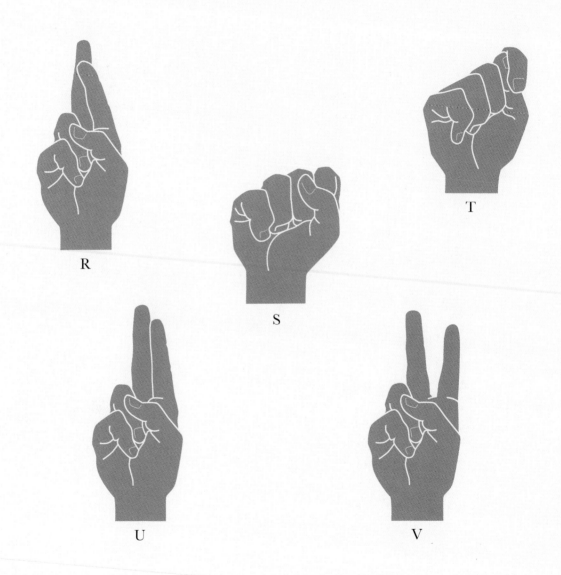

R

S

T

U

V

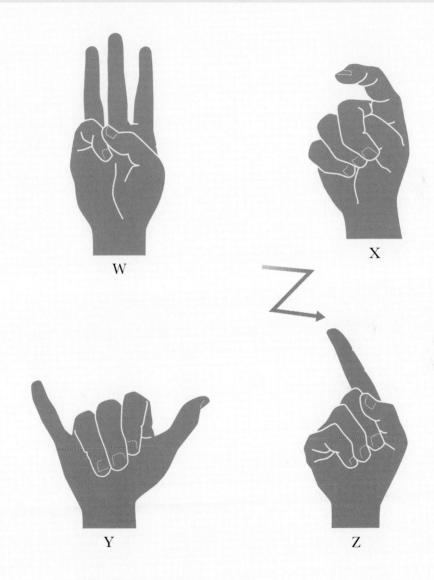

W

X

Y

Z

colors: red, blue, yellow

Colors are a fun way to expand your signing activities. Not only can you learn the colors themselves, but also apply them to countless objects and situations. Start with the three primary colors—red, yellow, and blue. Point out familiar objects and name its color. It can be helpful to introduce colors with either just a sample of the color itself or on an object he already knows the sign for.

red

Your index finger will move from your lower lip downward.

RECOMMENDED USAGE: For all things red, show your child this wonderful sign. To remember this sign, it may help that it reminds you of the red color of lips. Some good red things are ladybugs, fire trucks, strawberries, and roses.

everything is blue

One thing that children will often do is group similar things into one category, which is a common developmental step, but they will also often choose one label for everything in that category. This can happen with so many things, but one of the more common ones is color. My son learned the sign and word for "blue" first and applied it to all colors for a solid month before he got it all figured out correctly.

blue

Your "B" hand *(see page 101)* twists or shakes back and forth.

RECOMMENDED USAGE: This sign can be remembered by its handshape. "B" stands for "blue." The blue sky is a great thing to point out, as are morning glories, his favorite blue shirt, or maybe some stars you have colored blue in his coloring book.

yellow

Your "Y" hand *(see page 105)* twists or shakes back and forth.

RECOMMENDED USAGE: This is another sign that has a distinctive handshape. Look for yellows in your baby's world. The sun is a good choice, but obviously only in books or drawings. Flowers, lemons, and toy ducks are also great items to point out.

colors: green, orange, purple

The next step is to move on to the secondary colors—green, orange, and purple. You may have noticed that several color signs have the same position and movement but use a different handshape. The handshape may help you to remember the sign because it signifies the letter the color starts with. Blue, yellow, green, and purple are all very similar in this respect so it's possible your child may sign them similarly.

I want the green one!

Sometimes a child will want something but not know either the sign or the word for it. One of the most helpful aspects of knowing colors, whether they are in signs or words, is being able to ask, "What color?" If your child can name the color of the object he wants you will have a much greater chance of figuring it out.

green

Your "G" hand (*see page 102*) twists or shakes back and forth.

RECOMMENDED USAGE: The "G" handshape will help you remember this is the sign for "green." There are so many green things found in nature that this can be a great sign to teach on a neighborhood walk or a visit to the park. Grass, leaves, and some bugs are great starting points. Maybe you see a frog! You can also point out foods such as green beans.

orange

Open and close the space directly in front of your chin in a squeeze action.

RECOMMENDED USAGE: Think of squeezing an orange when you are learning and teaching this sign. An obvious starting point would be an actual orange or a glass of orange juice. You can then move on to orange flowers, basketballs, or an orange raincoat.

purple

Your "P" hand (*see page 103*) twists or shakes back and forth.

RECOMMENDED USAGE: Here is another color sign that is signified by its handshape. Purple can be found in lots of places. Violets, purple shoes, or a favorite character on television can inspire some "purple" signing.

colors: black, brown, pink

These color signs may not be as easily learned as the simpler colors. My children learned these soon after the others, but I waited until they understood the primary and secondary colors before introducing them.

black

With your index finger, draw a horizontal line across your forehead.

RECOMMENDED USAGE: This sign reminds me of someone who has black eyebrows. Help your child sign about the black cat or point out his black shoes. At night, he may sign "black" if he notices that the sky is dark.

signing white

White is found in abundance in nature—for example, in lots of animals. The sign for white is a motion that is similar to pulling your shirt away from your chest. Position your hand with fingers together pointing toward your chest and "pull" it outward. Think of wearing a white shirt when you sign this for the first time. You can help your child differentiate between a white dog and one of another color. You can also point out envelopes, clouds, snow, or mashed potatoes.

brown

The "B" hand *(see page 101)* slides down the side of your face, next to your mouth.

RECOMMENDED USAGE: The handshape of this sign will remind you of the word, and the fact that it is on your face instead of out in the typical color position tells you it isn't the sign for "blue." Lauren often confused this color with "black" but did in time sort it all out. It helped that our family pet, a dog, is coal black. Some brown things your child may be interested in signing about: bread, hair color, eye color, pets, and chocolate.

pink

Brush your lip with the second finger of the "P" hand *(see page 103)*.

RECOMMENDED USAGE: "Pink" is signed just like "red" except you use the "P" handshape to signify the difference. Try to point out pink flowers, mittens, frosting, or a pink toy.

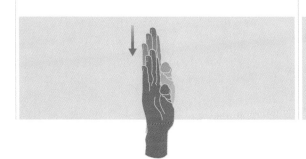

summing up progress

Congratulations! You have now learned many signs to introduce to your child. You will have noticed that I have divided the signs up into several chapters in order to construct a basic outline for you to follow, but you should feel free to pick and choose from the chapters to suit your needs and your child's.

your achievements

You now have the tools necessary to sign about a multitude of objects, people, actions, places, desires, activities, letters, and colors. You know the difference between High-Impact Signs and Need-Based Signs and have carefully selected a number of signs to teach to your child accordingly.

As you continue signing with your child, there is every chance that you are going to need a sign that is not illustrated in this book. I have provided a further resources section, giving you information on where to look for more signs *(see page 126)*.

"What I found to be the most amazing thing about having taught my daughter sign language was the ability to get inside her head and learn the associations and thoughts she had. One evening, she was watching me unload the dishwasher when she took a sippy cup with lid, placed a second lid on it, looked up at me and signed 'hat!' with a big grin on her face. What a generalization! If not for her signs, I would have assumed she was just stacking."

Eileen Landio, *speech language pathologist*

what's next?

The upcoming pages will show you where signing will take you as your child grows older. You also may be interested in meeting other parents and babies who are using sign language to facilitate early communication, and I will show you how you can do that.

As your child grows, you can continue to not only to sign with her, but to benefit from it as well.

combining signs

As your child's ability and enthusiasm for signing grows encourage him by beginning to combine some signs. The different color signs provide an excellent opportunity. If you show your child the color of a favorite animal or toy that he already knows the sign for, for example, you can easily combine the two signs together. He may also begin doing this on his own as he becomes surer of the signs he has learned.

10 signing and the older child

toddlerhood and beyond

Once your child starts speaking she will likely begin dropping signs like hot potatoes as she tries out words that she formerly signed. For many of you, signing will have served its purpose as a temporary, preverbal form of communication. Some, however, may wish to continue signing. Perhaps you have a close friend or relation who is deaf or have developed an interest in ASL through your baby-signing experiences. There are a few good reasons to continue signing with your child once she starts speaking.

why keep signing?
As I talked about earlier, children will commonly begin to combine signs with other signs as well as with spoken words as they grow and their communication abilities continue developing. This is an excellent opportunity to reinforce your child's

signing as well as for you to become motivated to learn even more signs. It can be very tempting to simply let the signing go, and it is perfectly fine to do so, especially if you were simply using sign language to span the gap between the preverbal and talking stages. However, since children do start speaking before they are completely done signing it really is a terrific opportunity to teach many more signs and even move into teaching ASL as a second language.

a real advantage
Your toddler may have already hit her signing explosion but that definitely isn't the end of the exploding part of it. After she grasps the concept of sign language and how effective a communication tool it is, she will really want to learn more signs for everything that she discovers

"Even before your baby says his first words—that milestone all we parents treasure—he may actually invent a few 'words' of his own. Even though these aren't actual words per se, you can tell your tot thinks of them as words because he uses them consistently and in the same context."

Robert E. Owens, Jr., Ph.D., *Help Your Baby Talk*

or does on a daily basis. Once a child has had the benefit of signing from a young age, she is more apt to pick up additional signs and you can really use that to her advantage. Also, older children have a really fantastic ability to pick up new things—sign language included.

speech delay

Please consult your pediatrician if you have any questions or concerns regarding your child's development—whether it is language related or not. However, one thing to keep in mind is that by 24 months children will likely be speaking approximately 50 words and beginning to combine them in two-word sentences. This is not a definite rule, only a general guideline, but if your child isn't anywhere near these goals consider bringing it up with her physician.

When a child is too distressed to speak, signing can come in very handy.

engaging the older signer

Whether your child is an established signer or not, there are a number of ways to engage her with signing activities and to continue her signing education—along with yours. These activities are appropriate for toddlers upward, but you can certainly include your younger baby. Even though she may not be signing a lot at this point, any signing you do will definitely benefit her.

take a walk

Taking a nature walk with your child is a great idea at any time, but if you take advantage of the experience by teaching signs as you go along, there is an even greater benefit. Incorporate what you see into a running dialogue with your child (with ample questions and appropriate pauses so she can answer you and communicate ideas of her own). Point out

Holidays are a fantastic time to introduce or reinforce sign language.

"Parents who continue to use signs beyond the early word phase have children who continue to sign while they're speaking. These parents can also invite children to sign when words are unclear. These practices give parents multiple cues to better understand their child's speech."

Dr. Michelle Anthony and Dr. Reyna Lindert,
Signing Smart with Babies and Toddlers: A Parent's Strategy and Activity Guide

what you see with its accompanying sign (for example, "flower," "tree," "dog") and see if she is interested in describing colors or objects to you.

party time

Parties and holidays are excellent opportunities to practice signing with your child. From the special food to the party itself, your child will be dazzled by the events. Some signs to learn before your family gathering might be: "family," "party," "cake," "light," "ice cream," and many more. Stay close to your child and watch for the right moment to engage her with a new sign. Certain elements of holidays are also good signs to learn, and can go along with introducing your child to your culture or religion.

books

Books are a great way to interact with your child and assist her mental development and they are also full of signing opportunities. You will probably find appropriate and interesting subject matter to sign about in your child's books. Point out objects and their colors, and as your child grows, begin pointing out the letters and help her form those signs if she will let you. If you have signed with a particular book often enough, your child may want to look at the book by herself, and if you're lucky you might catch her signing to herself as she leafs through.

at the zoo

Undeniably the zoo is one of the best places to expose your child to many signs all in one day. Be sure to bring along a sign-language dictionary or learn enough wild and domestic animal signs to keep your child satisfied. Be prepared for a little bit of confusion when you confront some not-so-common animals, such as the okapi, which your child may think is a zebra or a horse, but is actually a member of the giraffe family.

signing past preschool

In addition to taking advantage of special outings or activities to further encourage the use of sign language, you can maintain your signing habits when your child is older.

Keeping up with sign language even after your child has mastered a great number of spoken words is a great idea because not only will your child be able to communicate with deaf friends at her playgroup or school but you will have your own way of communicating with her without saying a word.

the speaking child

Teaching sign language after a child is speaking on a regular basis is similar to teaching a baby sign language, only you have to be a bit more motivated. Often, once a baby begins talking, she will naturally drop each sign as she begins to say the word, and parents fall out of the habit of signing with their child for the simple reason that it is no longer needed for communication. Many

(if not most) parents sign with their young babies as a temporary exercise, but there are quite a few who would like to continue to do so for the above-mentioned reasons.

keep on signing

If you learn ASL (by taking a class or through contact with a deaf friend or family member) it will become second nature to speak with your hands in addition to using your voice. Just as with any second language, your child will pick up ASL as she would a spoken language as long as you or other family members use it consistently. It also helps if she sees you using the signs as you talk with others as well as with her.

If you don't want to invest time and energy in actually learning ASL you can still pick and choose important words to sign (just as you do when signing to a baby or a toddler). Your child will still get a lot of benefits from this and she will probably really enjoy it too.

Signing "potty" is so much better than saying, "Poopie!" as loud as he can.

taking a class

If you are going to continue signing with your child past the toddler and preschool years, you might consider taking a sign-language class so you can learn the proper grammar and context of a signed language such as ASL. Look for local continuing education classes through a nearby college or see if there are courses offered through your community center. Some places even offer sign-language classes for children.

branching out

meeting fellow signers

It is awesome to sign with your baby and it's terrific to share that with friends and family members. However, even if they are supportive, they might not be signing with their babies, and there is something wonderful about connecting with another parent who is a signer.

the benefits

Meeting other signing parents can have many benefits. When you get together with them you might be really encouraged by their progress or by your mutual resolve to sign with your baby. You can trade hints and strategies and let them know what works for your family. It is also a lot of fun to see what signs their child knows and is working on— chances are, they are not the same ones your family knows, so there is an opportunity to learn new signs as well. You might already participate in a playgroup with your child. If you do, poll the other parents and see if anyone else is signing with their baby. You might even notice that some of the children are using signs. If you have older children who attend school, seek out other parents who also have younger children and ask them if they are signing with them.

Connecting with other parents is a pleasure, especially when you have signing with babies in common.

say hi

If you are more adventurous, you can seek out people who you don't know but may be familiar to you—perhaps you see the same mother and baby at the store each week, or at the library with her toddler each time you go. The playground or park is also a common meeting place for parents who aren't friends yet.

Another thing to keep in mind: remember when you were expecting your baby and suddenly you noticed pregnant women and babies everywhere you went? That may hold true for signing with babies as well. You are naturally more aware of sign language and may see it more often as you are out. As the popularity of signing with babies continues to increase, this may happen even more regularly. You can take advantage of your signing knowledge and, if interested, you may decide to introduce yourself to some new people. You also may be approached by families who don't sign with their baby but are curious about the process.

new friendships

Establishing contact with other signing parents certainly has its merits in and of itself, but it can also be a really good way for you and your child to make new friends. You automatically have something in common, which can make it easy to spark up conversation. Having a common goal (that is, signing with your child) won't guarantee a lifetime friendship but it can definitely begin one!

finding a signing playgroup

In addition to trying to find other signing parents through your own social contacts, you also have the option of looking for a playgroup or even a class that is centered on signing with babies.

ask around

It may be really easy to find a signing playgroup or it may take a bit of research. It depends on how much advertising the group is able to do. I suggest asking other parents that you know who already sign with their babies. Did they take a class? Do they know of a group? Another resource might be your local school district. Phone the main office and ask if the people there know of any classes offered, either through their departments or private individuals. If you have no luck, try a neighboring school district, particularly if it serves a larger city.

Local baby or child-centered stores (such as children's bookstores, resale clothing shops, and specialty toy stores) may either have classes in-store or may have a bulletin board where instructors post announcements. Check with the owner or other employees to see if they know of anything. Another place you could check might be your pediatrician's office. Check with either the staff or the other parents in the waiting room (preferably the well side, if there is one).

spread the word

Also, you can scan your local paper and any local parenting magazines or publications. Let others know that you are looking for a group like this and they may have information or resources you may not have access to.

Finding a group may be the hard part, but attending, having fun, and learning are all easy!

Imagine the possibilities when you get together with other signing families.

national signing groups

There are many different companies that offer workshops, classes, or playgroups for signing babies and their parents. They have websites and you can search for a local class that way. Please see Further Reading, Websites (*page 126*) to find out more about them. Most if not all cost money, but it can be a worthwhile investment if you would like to connect with other parents as well as see baby signing demonstrated in person.

starting your own group

If you haven't had any success finding an already established playgroup, you might be inspired to start your own. This can be rewarding and a lot of fun, but it does take some planning and hard work.

motivation and planning

The first thing you will need for this project is a healthy dose of motivation. If your desire to find signing parents is strong then this may be all that you need to begin! Having support from family and friends is really important as well, and may lead you to resources and opportunities that you may not have otherwise known about.

Next, you will need to begin planning the meetings. Concentrate first on the concrete details, such as the meeting day and time. Do you want to relegate it to the evenings or weekends, to include as many parents as possible? Or, if you are a stay-at-home mom, do you want to focus on a time during the week? Also consider the frequency of the meetings. Would once a month be enough, or would weekly get-togethers be better?

setting goals

Then consider what the goal of your meetings will be. Do you want to simply provide somewhere for mutual support for people who sign with babies, where you can meet, hang out, and share your progress and goals while your kids play? Or do you want to actually show parents what you have learned and create more of a learning environment? Deciding this now will make advertising and running the group a good deal easier in the future.

Finding a place to meet may be the biggest hurdle you face. If you are going to be offering free meetings, consider a local library or a church. Your home is also an option if you feel comfortable giving out your home address and telephone number. You might check with local children's stores to see whether they would offer to host you. Other options might be a shopping mall or a children's park.

Hanging up flyers around town is a great place to begin finding other signing families.

advertise

For advertising, whip up a flyer on your computer's word processing program and distribute it all over town. Look for bulletin boards at grocery stores, daycare centers, shopping malls, and wherever else you can think of. Try to focus on places where parents may go or shop on a regular basis. Be sure to take your own tape and tacks, just in case nothing is provided for you, and ask permission first if there is no immediately obvious place to attach flyers. Include a phone number or an email address so interested people can contact you. Also, if it's free, include FREE in huge letters.

Starting your own group can be so much fun!

free advertising resources

Generally, advertising isn't cheap, but you may find some places to advertise that are completely free. The top suggestions are your local paper and your local cable company or television station. See if the paper has a community calendar listing, or if the cable company has any free advertising time on a channel. You may be able to go on camera to promote your upcoming meetings.

further reading, websites

Do you want to start your own signing business?

You may be so inspired by signing with your own children that you would like to have the tools, resources, and support to start teaching signing to other parents, caregivers, and babies. Check the books and websites on this page for information on where to begin.

General Resources

Signing with Your Baby
www.signingbaby.com
Author's site: articles, signing baby photos, information, store, and more

Signing with Your Baby
Yahoo Group
http://groups.yahoo.com/groups/signingbaby
Online and email discussion group for signing with babies (author-led)

ASL Online Dictionaries

Communication Technology Laboratory, Michigan State University
http://commtechlab.msu.edu/sites/aslweb/browser.htm

Educational resource with over 8,000 signs
www.aslpro.com

ASL information, lessons, and dictionary
www.lifeprint.com

Signing Baby Companies
(to find classes or become an instructor)

Baby Signs
www.babysigns.com

Sign2Me
www.sign2me.com

Signing Smart
www.signingsmart.com

Video/DVD

Baby Einstein—Baby Wordsworth—First Words—Around the House
(Buena Vista Home Video)

Baby See 'n' Sign (Volumes I and II)
(Kronz Kids Productions)

My Baby Can Talk—First Signs
(Baby Hands Productions)

Signing Time! Volumes 1–6
Baby Signing Time! Volumes 1 and 2
(Two Little Hands Productions)

Treasure Chest: Toys and Signs
Auraria Media Center
(Signing Smart product)

Books

Baby's First Signs by Kim Votry and Curt Waller (Gallaudet University Press, 2001)

Baby Sign Language Basics by Monta Briant (Hay House, 2004)

Baby Signs: How to Talk with Your Baby Before Your Baby Can Talk by Dr. Linda Acredolo and Dr. Susan Goodwyn (McGraw-Hill, 2002)

Dancing with Words: Signing for Hearing Children's Literacy by Marilyn Daniels (Bergin & Garvey Paperback, 2001)

First Signs by Stanley Collins (Garlic Press, 2001)

Help Your Baby to Talk by Robert E. Owens, Jr., Ph.D. (Penguin, 2004)

Look Who's Talking! by Laura Dyer, M.C.D., (Meadowbrook Press, 2004)

Sign with Your Baby by Dr. Joseph Garcia (Northlight Communications, 2004)

Signing Smart with Babies and Toddlers: A Parent's Strategy and Activity Guide by Dr. Michelle Anthony and Dr. Reyna Lindert (St. Martin's Griffin, 2005)

Teach Your Tot to Sign: The Parents' Guide to American Sign Language by Stacy Thompson (Gallaudet University Press, 2005)

index

A

ABCs 83
a–z 100–105
Acredolo, Dr. Linda 12,
40
advertising 125
again 64
all done 35, 79
alphabet song 100
American Psychological
Association 13
American Sign Language
(ASL) 10–11, 14–15,
39, 49, 92, 114, 118–19
Anderson, Dr. Diane 13
Anthony, Dr. Michelle 13,
19, 86
apple 88
attention 19

B

Baby Signs, Inc. 12
babysitters 39, 46–47,
50, 69
bath 23, 35
bear 60
bedtime 23
bird 33
black 110
blue 107
boat 55
body language 21
books 39, 49, 54, 117
bread 59

brown 111
brush teeth 86

C

cake 91
candy 89
car 55
caregivers 48–49
cat 33
change 57
classes 119, 122–23
cold 30
colors 83, 106–11
combining signs 70–75,
113
consistency 14, 18, 43,
46–47, 49, 92
context 43–45
cookie 58
cow 61
cracker 59

D

daycare 10, 39, 46, 48–49,
69
diaper 56
dictionaries 11, 51, 117,
126
dirty 57
dog 32
down 65
drink 31
duck 93

E

eat 27
education 69
elephant 61
expressive language 14, 16

F

fall down 67
family 50–51, 80–81,
84–85
fan 38
father 37
fish 34
flower 37
friendships 121

G

games 82–83
giraffe 62
goal-setting 124
Goodwyn, Dr. Susan 12
grandfather 85
grandmother 84
grandparents 50–51,
84–85
grapes 89
green 108

H

handedness 25
help 28, 76, 78
high-impact signs 19, 24,
26, 32, 39, 94, 112

home 95
horse 63
hot 29
hurt 29

I

ice cream 90
in/into 68
in-laws 50–51, 80, 84
interpretation 14

K

key signs 78

L

language development 9,
13–17, 40, 70–73, 83,
114–15
letters 83, 100–105
light 38
Lindert, Dr. Reyna 13,
19, 86
lion 92

M

me/mine 99
mealtimes 22
milk 26

index

N

need-based signs 19, 24, 26, 39, 112
new babies 80–81
no 40

O

off 95
on 94
orange 109
out 68
outside 87

P

party 91, 117
patience 24
pink 111
planning 124
play 87
playgroups 120, 122–25
please 79, 98
purple 109

R

receptive language 16
red 106
research 12–13, 122

S

secret languages 80
shoes 96
sibling bonding 80–81
signed languages 11

signing explosion 17
Signing Smart 13, 86
sitting up 20
socks 97
stress 76–77

T

tantrums 76–81
telegraphic speech 74–75
thank you 99
tiger 93
timeline 15
tree 97
troubleshooting 39–45

U

up 65

W

walks 116–17
want 66
water 31
websites 8, 10, 123, 126
where 67
white 110

Y

yelling 41
yellow 107

Z

zoos 60, 117

First and foremost, I would like to thank my husband, Kevin, for his valuable help during the writing of this book. He is a great partner, friend, and supporter, and is a wonderful father.

I would also like to thank my parents and my mother-in-law for their support and for being excellent signing grandparents. My friend Sarah provided (as she always does) a much-needed ear and was extremely encouraging (I couldn't ask for a better friend). Corrie, Robin, Erika, and the "private private" crew were also so helpful.

Thanks also go to the parents who helped me with this book—those who contributed directly and those who are simply fabulous signing parents. Your dedication and experiences continue to move me on a daily basis.

Thanks also go to the experts on signing with babies whose works I consulted—Dr. Michelle Anthony, Dr. Reyna Lindert, Dr. Linda Acredolo, Dr. Susan Goodwyn, and Dr. Joseph Garcia. Your research, commitment, and hard work are so appreciated among so many signing families. Special thanks go to Dr. Anthony and Dr. Acredolo for their direct help and guidance.

My greatest inspiration, however, comes from my three children—Dagan, Corbin, and Lauren. You continue to amaze me every day with your beauty and intelligence. Thank you for being my babies.

Dedicated to the memory of
JORDANA ROSE ROSS
07/04/04 – 06/24/05